**Butterworths
Inheritance Tax
Guide**

Butterworths Inheritance Tax Guide

C. V. Margrave-Jones MA, LLM(Cantab);
Solicitor,
Lecturer in Law,
University College of Wales,
Aberystwyth

London ·Butterworths · 1986

United Kingdom	Butterworth & Co (Publishers) Ltd, 88 Kingsway, LONDON WC2B 6AB and 61A North Castle Street, EDINBURGH EH2 3LJ
Australia	Butterworths Pty Ltd, SYDNEY, MELBOURNE, BRISBANE, ADELAIDE, PERTH, CANBERRA and HOBART
Canada	Butterworths. A division of Reed Inc., TORONTO and VANCOUVER
New Zealand	Butterworths of New Zealand Ltd, WELLINGTON and AUCKLAND
Singapore	Butterworth & Co (Asia) Pte Ltd, SINGAPORE
South Africa	Butterworth Publishers (Pty) Ltd, DURBAN and PRETORIA
USA	Butterworth Legal Publishers, ST PAUL, Minnesota, SEATTLE, Washington, BOSTON, Massachusetts, AUSTIN, Texas and D & S Publishers, CLEARWATER, Florida

British Library Cataloguing in Publication Data
Margrave-Jones, C.V.
  Butterworths' inheritance tax guide
  1. Inheritance and transfer tax — England 2. Tax planning — England
  I. Title
  336.2'76   KD5560

ISBN 0 406 50034 7

Typeset by Kerrypress Ltd, Luton
Printed by Biddles of Guildford

Preface

As the title of this book suggests, it is intended primarily as a practical guide to inheritance tax. Inheritance tax combines aspects of both capital transfer tax and estate duty which preceded it. Capital transfer tax swept away estate duty in the Finance Act 1975, which was consolidated in the Capital Transfer Tax Act 1984, renamed the Inheritance Tax Act 1984 by the FA 1986. Apart, however, from the renaming of the tax as inheritance tax and the introduction of the new category of potentially exempt transfers, the essential structure of the 1984 Act has been retained. However, certain features of estate duty, in particular the gifts with reservation provisions, were re-introduced which, it is anticipated, will create many problems for practitioners and their clients.

This book, in considering the basic principles of inheritance tax, is aimed at three classes of readers. First, those encountering inheritance tax for the first time should find it helpful as an introduction to the tax. Secondly, those readers who have been reared on capital transfer tax will hopefully find the book useful in dealing with the transition from capital transfer tax to inheritance tax: in particular the book stresses, where appropriate, the dangers of applying certain tax planning ideas appropriate to capital transfer tax, which may prove to be pitfalls when applied to inheritance tax. Finally, it is hoped that the book will be useful to those who, like myself, have practised under the estate duty and the capital transfer tax regimes: the book considers the re-introduced estate duty provisions and emphasises where these have been modified under the new tax.

As a busy practitioner myself, often working in close conjunction with the accountancy profession, I am very conscious of the fact that many readers, already familiar with capital transfer tax, may initially only wish to be rapidly apprised of the changes effected by the FA 1986. This objective may be achieved by first reading Chapter 2 which incorporates most of the new features, and then referring to Appendix A which will direct the reader to the remaining changes appearing in this Guide.

From the taxpayer's point of view, inheritance tax combines many of the virtues of capital transfer tax (in particular the total spouse exemption and the possibility of deeds of variation which were not available under estate duty) and features of estate duty, in particular the exemption for tax where the donor survives seven years. With proper professional advice and planning, the new tax is, therefore, potentially a more voluntary tax than was estate duty in its final form; the consequences of not taking such advice may prove disastrous. This book emphasises, with examples, where these difficulties are likely to be encountered following the FA 1986.

This Guide could not have been written within the stringent timetable requested but for the speed and skill of my secretary, Valerie Cosgrave, in transcribing the manuscript while at the same time appeasing clients during my absences from the office!

The law is stated as at 1 August 1986.

Clive V. Margrave-Jones

Contents

Contents

Table of Statutes

Table of Cases

Introduction

0.01 There are now only three duties or taxes imposed on death which are likely to be of any relevance: estate duty, applying to estates of persons dying before 13 March 1975; capital transfer tax in respect of lifetime gifts made after 26 March 1974 but before 18 March 1986, and imposed on estates of persons dying before that date; and inheritance tax in respect of a limited class of lifetime gifts and estates of persons dying after 17 March 1986.

ESTATE DUTY

0.02 This duty had survived until 1975, virtually unchanged in principle since Sir William Harcourt's revision of 1894. While this duty no longer arises in respect of estates of persons dying after 12 March 1975, it may still be of relevance in three respects:

(1) *Persons dying before 13 March 1975.*   Where such estates have not yet been fully administered, estate duty may still be payable. In practice, this situation may arise more often than one would anticipate where, for example, the main asset is the principal residence, and the surviving spouse or another member of the family has merely continued to live in the property without taking out a grant of representation.

(2) *Interests in expectancy.*   There may be a potential charge to duty where a person dying before 13 March 1975 held an interest in expectancy which has not fallen into possession and an election was made to postpone the payment of tax until such time as the interest fell into possession. When the interest falls into possession, duty will be charged on that interest at the appropriate rate and aggregated with the original estate. Such interests do not now normally attract a charge to tax.

(3) *Limited interest of spouse exemption.*   Under the estate duty provisions, where there is a limited interest, usually a life interest, to a spouse with remainders over, estate duty was paid on the first death, but no estate duty (or capital transfer tax or inheritance tax) becomes payable on the death of the surviving

1

spouse. The surviving spouse could be given a special power of appointment, for example among the children, without loss of the exemption, but the exemption would be lost if the surviving spouse was at any time during the continuance of the settlement competent to dispose of the property, such as by a general power of appointment. One particular difficulty that may arise here is where the surviving spouse has a life interest but powers are given to the trustees to advance moneys to the life tenant out of the capital of the trust fund. If the surviving spouse becomes the sole surviving executor or trustee and therefore becomes capable of exercising this power in her favour, then the relief is lost. A well-drawn power would avoid this potential danger by providing that the power could not be exercised unless there were at least two trustees or a trust corporation to exercise it, but sometimes this provision was omitted in the drafting. It is therefore important that, where such a situation still exists, the surviving spouse never becomes the sole executor or trustee.

0.03 This continuing estate duty exemption in the case of a surviving spouse who has a limited life interest is of extreme importance, because not only is no tax payable on the death of the surviving spouse, but also the trust fund is not aggregated with the surviving spouse's estate. Further, the benefit of these provisions is generally compounded by the fact that, although no inheritance tax will now be paid on the termination of the life interest, there will still be a capital gains tax uplift of the trust assets on the death of the life tenant, therefore justifying as high a value as possible as can be negotiated on the value of the trust funds.

CAPITAL TRANSFER TAX

0.04 This tax has been described as a re-enactment of the old estate duty provisions with 'gifts tax sections welded on the front end, but with no accession element' (Sabine *A History of Taxation*). This is perhaps an unfair judgment on the FA 1975, which introduced the new notion of a transfer of value. Capital transfer tax applied to lifetime transfers made after 26 March 1974 and on death on or after 13 March 1975 (the date the FA 1975 received Royal assent). A death before 13 March 1975 attracted estate duty as did lifetime transfers after 26 March 1974 if the transferor died before 13 March 1975.

0.05 Estate duty was always regarded as a voluntary tax in that it could be avoided by making lifetime gifts and surviving that gift by a period of years, which in the final form of the tax was seven years. The objective of capital transfer tax was to ensure that the tax could not be so easily avoided, by taxing lifetime gifts and cumulating all chargeable gifts with the estate of the deceased for ascertaining the final rate of tax on death. When the tax was initially introduced, it virtually achieved its object as the lower lifetime rates only applied up to a relatively low limit and the cumulation of gifts applied throughout one's lifetime.

0.06 These stringent provisions were substantially eroded when the lifetime rates were reduced to half the death rates throughout the scale and the cumulation period reduced to ten years. A further deterrent to lifetime gifts was the potential capital gains tax charge on the donor, a disincentive that was removed by the FA 1981, which allowed hold-over of the gain.

INHERITANCE TAX

The FA 1986

0.07 Capital transfer tax has now been compulsorily renamed as inheritance tax and the Capital Transfer Tax Act 1984 has now been given the optional, alternative, title of 'the Inheritance Tax Act 1984'. Throughout this Guide a reference to the 1984 Act is to the Inheritance Tax Act 1984, and a reference to a section is to the section in that Act, unless otherwise indicated. The changes in the rules for charging tax are effective on and after 18 March 1986. The FA 1986 has achieved the change in tax mainly by inserting additional provisions in the 1984 Act which remains therefore the principal Act for the charge to inheritance tax.

Potentially exempt transfers

0.08 Inheritance tax has now reverted to the principle of charging lifetime gifts only if made in the period of seven years before the deceased's death, with certain exceptions. This has been achieved by introducing a new class of transfers of value known as potentially exempt transfers. Such transfers will be exempt from tax if made within seven years from the date of death of the deceased and provided no benefit has been reserved to the donor. If the deceased dies within seven years of the gift, it becomes a chargeable transfer. Not all transfers of value qualify as potentially exempt transfers but principally only those made between individuals or by an individual into an accumulation or maintenance trust or into a trust for the disabled.

3

Lifetime chargeable transfers

0.09 Other transfers of value which are not potentially exempt transfers of value, in this Guide referred to as lifetime chargeable transfers, will be charged tax as lifetime transfers of value as they were under capital transfer tax, except that the period of cumulation has now been reduced from ten to seven years. The structure of the 1984 Act has therefore been retained.

Reintroduction of gifts with reservation

0.10 However, while the FA 1986 has introduced the concessions of partially exempt transfers and reduced the cumulation period to seven years, it has endeavoured to graft on to capital transfer tax, somewhat unsatisfactorily, various features of estate duty, in particular the new provisions relating to gifts of property subject to a reservation. It is anticipated that these provisions will cause acute problems, as illustrated by some of the examples given in the ensuing chapters, in particular Chapter 2.

'Artificial debts'

0.11 With the reintroduction of the rules relating to property subject to a reservation, it has also been necessary to reintroduce provisions to disallow certain debts as an anti-avoidance measure. It is anticipated that these new provisions will also create problems, in contrast to the relative freedom under capital transfer tax of sales and loan-backs. These problems are anticipated in Chapter 6.

Curtailment of business property and agricultural property reliefs

0.12 These substantial reliefs afforded to business and agricultural properties have been curtailed by requiring the transferee to continue to own and qualify for these reliefs up to seven years before the transferor's death. Some of the difficulties anticipated in this area are illustrated in Chapter 7.

Allocation of exemptions

0.13 The method of allocation of exemptions as they apply to business property relief and agricultural property relief has been revised; they cannot now be utilised to enhance the relief as previously. These new provisions and worked examples are also contained in Chapter 7.

Settled Property

0.14 The concept of a transfer of value, which is any disposition by which the value of a person's estate is reduced, has been retained for inheritance tax. A change in the beneficial enjoyment in possession in settled funds is not strictly a transfer of value, but it is effectively treated as one. This will arise where, for example, a life interest comes to an end. When the beneficial interest in possession changes, there is a charge to tax as if there had been a transfer of value of the property in which the interest subsisted. Special rules apply to discretionary settlements where no person is entitled to an interest in possession. These are considered in Chapter 8.

Companies

0.15 A company is not liable to inheritance tax when it makes a disposition of its own assets, as the tax is only chargeable on dispositions by individuals. While the company may not be charged to tax, if it is a close company, the individual participants will be treated as having made a transfer of value. Further, if there is an alteration in the capital structure of the company which varies the value of the interests of the participants, this is treated as a transfer of value between the participants themselves. These provisions are very briefly considered in Chapter 3.

0.16 As a transfer to a company or, in the situations outlined, by a company, is not a potentially exempt transfer, there is now a deterrent against using companies as a method of transferring capital.

Exemptions

0.17 The 1984 Act contains three principal methods of providing for exemption from liability to inheritance tax:

(1) *Dispositions which are not transfers of value.* A certain category of dispositions are declared not to be transfers of value. Such dispositions include commercial transactions which are not intended to confer any gratuitous benefit on any person, various dispositions for maintenance of the transferor's family and certain other dispositions set out in the Act. While these dispositions result in a loss to the transferor's estate, they do not attract inheritance tax as they are not transfers of value.

(2) *Excluded property.* Dispositions of excluded property are transfers of value, but no account is taken of the value which therefore does not form part of the transferor's estate. The

principal categories of excluded property are reversionary interests and assets situate abroad belonging to persons not domiciled in the UK.

(3) *Exempt transfers.* Certain dispositions which are transfers of value and which would otherwise be chargeable transfers are given exemption. The exemption may be given on the basis of the character of the transferee, such as gifts to spouses or to a charity, or on the basis of a limited nature of a lifetime transfer, such as the annual exemption, marriage gifts, etc. Certain other transfers, such as gifts for national purposes and public benefit, are given conditional exemption from tax provided undertakings given with regard to them are fulfilled.

Reliefs

0.18 A relief from tax, as opposed to an exemption, may be given in a number of ways:

(1) *Reduction in value.* Some reliefs provide that there is a reduction in value in the assets transferred. This applies, for example, to the agricultural value of agricultural land and business property whereby the value of the asset is reduced for tax purposes. By reducing the value of the asset this benefits all assets which are cumulated or aggregated with the estate.

(2) *Tapered relief on lifetime transfers.* Other reliefs take the form of a reduction in the rate of tax, such as the tapered relief given for lifetime transfers made between three and seven years before the date of death. The effect of this relief is to reduce the tax payable on those particular transfers, but does not reduce the value for the purpose of cumulation.

(3) *Tax credit.* Another form of relief gives a credit against tax falling due, such as with quick succession relief and double taxation relief. Once again the full value transferred is cumulated or aggregated with the estate and merely a reduced amount of tax is payable by reason of the credit.

(4) *Property left out of account.* It may be provided that the particular property is to be left out of account, such as in the case of growing timber.

Post-death variations

0.19 Under the FA 1975, for the first time it became possible by agreement among the beneficiaries to vary the distribution of an estate after death (there were certain limitations until the FA 1977). Indeed it is now normal practice when administering an estate to consider whether any variation in the distribution of the estate should be made. It is also now not an infrequent practice to make a succession of variations during the period of two years following the death.

Curtailments

0.20 Often the principal or sole purpose of effecting a variation or series of variations is to mitigate the tax liability on the deceased's estate or the potential tax liability on a beneficiary's estate. Some doubt has been raised as to the extent to which post-death variations have now been curtailed by the decision of the House of Lords in *Ramsey v IRC*, as more recently developed in *Furniss v Dawson*. Initially it was felt that the new doctrine did not apply to inheritance tax, but present indications are that it applies to all taxes. The implications of this new doctrine are considered briefly in the final chapter.

Principal changes effected by the FA 1986

0.21 The reader who is already familiar with capital transfer tax and who wishes to be apprised of the recent changes should first read Chapter 2, which will acquaint him with the principal changes; if he then refers to Appendix A, this will direct him to the remaining changes appearing in this Guide.

Political foresight

0.22 The power of inherited wealth makes the taxation of it politically sensitive. Even in the estate duty era it was not always easy to anticipate the effect of political changes, except possibly to foresee that the avoidance of tax by using a discretionary trust could not continue for ever and to anticipate the lengthening of the period a donee had to survive a gift to avoid estate duty.

0.23 Following the new restrictions imposed in the FA 1986, not many changes would have to be effected to make inheritance tax a stringent tax once again. Simply lengthening the cumulation period and the periods of tapered relief would achieve this, possibly combined with the reintroduction of a progressively higher charge on lifetime transfers.

0.24 However, perhaps inheritance tax will be left as it is and instead a wealth tax introduced, which would be the subject matter of another book!

CHAPTER 1

The charge of inheritance tax

Introduction

1.01   Inheritance tax is charged on a chargeable transfer made after 17 March 1986. Although the tax has been re-named, the basic structure of the tax remains the same as that contained in the Capital Transfer Tax Act 1984, now optionally re-named the Inheritance Tax Act 1984 (FA 1986, s 101).

The principle of cumulation (s 7)

1.02   The principle of cumulation has been retained. This principle requires that the tax on the present transfer must take account of chargeable transfers already made by the transferor in the preceding seven years; equally, subsequent transfers within seven years of the present transfer will take account of the present transfer. Finally, on death, all chargeable transfers made within seven years of the death are cumulated with the transferor's estate and any other assets charged at that time. This principle is considered in greater detail at para **9.02**.

1.03   Inheritance tax is charged on the value transferred by a chargeable transfer of value made by an individual and which is not an exempt transfer (s 1).

A TRANSFER OF VALUE (s 3)

Definition

1.04   A transfer of value is any disposition made by an individual as a result of which the value of his estate immediately after the disposition is less than it would have been but for the disposition. The net loss to the estate is therefore the value transferred. On death a person is deemed to have made a transfer of value equal to the value of his estate immediately before his death.

Meaning of disposition

1.05 The word 'disposition' used in s 3 is not defined in the 1984 Act, although it includes a disposition effected by associated operations (see para **1.24** below). It is therefore an ordinary word capable of a very wide meaning which includes the transfer of assets, payment of money and the creation of a settlement. It should be distinguished from the word 'disposal' used in capital gains tax legislation.

Destruction of an asset

1.06 In view of the wide meaning of disposition, it would seem to include a destruction of an asset. The 1984 Act does not specifically require a transferee, only a disposition resulting in a loss to the transferor's estate. If that interpretation is correct, the deliberate (or for that matter accidental) destruction of an asset, such as destroying a valuable picture, would appear to be a disposition resulting in a loss to the estate.

Omission to exercise a right (s 3(3))

1.07 Where the value of a person's estate is diminished and that of another person's estate is increased by the first person's omission to exercise a right, he is treated as having made a disposition at the time (or latest time) when he could have exercised the right unless it is shown that the omission was not deliberate.

Requirement to increase another person's estate

1.08 To establish that there has been a transfer of value, normally one only looks at the net loss to the transferor's estate and not the gain to the transferee's estate. However, for an omission to act to be treated as a disposition resulting in a loss to the transferor's estate, it is necessary that another person's estate, or a settled property in which no interest in possession subsists, is increased by the omission to act.

1.09 An example of such an omission would be the failure by a landlord to exercise a rent review clause, which would result in increasing the value of the tenant's interest in the lease. Similarly, a failure to take up a favourable rights issue which leads to the increase in the value of the holding of the remaining shareholders would be such an omission within the meaning of the section. Likewise, allowing a debt to become statute-barred would be an omission to act. However, there is a proviso that an omission will not be treated as a disposition if the omission was not deliberate, but the burden of proving that the omission was not deliberate is on the transferor.

Loss to the transferor's estate

1.10 A mere omission in itself resulting in a benefit to another person's estate is not a transfer of value unless there is a loss to the transferor's estate. This may be a matter of general law. If, for example, a father and son go into a shop and the father sees a vase, which he recognises as being an original Ming, for sale at £100, whereas its true value is £100,000, if he omits to buy it but suggests to his son that he might buy it, it would not be a transfer of value unless the vase formed part of the father's estate. This would be a question of the general law. If the father gave the son £100 with which to purchase the vase, then he has made a transfer of value of £100; alternatively, if the father had purchased the vase and then immediately handed it to his son, then the loss to his estate would have been the true value of the vase.

Meaning of estate (s 5)

1.11 For the purpose of inheritance tax, a person's estate has an extended meaning and is the total of all the following:

(1) *Assets to which a person is beneficially entitled.* Such assets would include any claims which may be made by his personal representatives (such as damages for loss of expectation of life) but not claims which a person or his personal representatives cannot enforce, such as gaming winnings or payments made to the estate at the discretion of the trustees of a superannuation scheme. A claim for damages under the Fatal Accident Acts is a claim made by the deceased's dependants in their own right and does not therefore form part of the deceased's estate.

(2) *Interests in possession.* A person beneficially entitled to an interest in possession in settled property is treated as being beneficially entitled to the property in which the interest subsists and not merely the interest itself (s 49(1)). Therefore, if a deceased was a life tenant in settled property consisting of assets worth £100,000 and the life tenant's own estate consists of £50,000, then the trust funds in the free estate are aggregated together and tax will be payable on a total estate of £150,000 which will be apportioned rateably between the trust and the free estate.

(3) *General power of appointment.* Where a person has a general power of appointment to dispose of any property (other than

settled property, such as a power of appointment conferred on the trustees of a discretionary trust) he is treated as being beneficially entitled to that property. For this purpose a general power is one enabling the person by whom it is exercisable to appoint or dispose of property as he thinks fit.

The loss to the estate

1.12 The value transferred is the net loss to the estate of the transferor and does not therefore necessarily bear any relationship to the benefit received by his transferee. To assess the loss to the estate one simply values the estate of the transferor before and after the disposition and it is the net difference which represents the loss to the estate.

1.13 Consequently, the benefit received by the transferee is not taken into account. As an illustration of this principle, if the transferor has a pair of pictures individually worth £5,000 each, but as a pair worth £20,000, and he gives away one of the pictures, the loss to his estate is £15,000 as he is now only left with a picture worth £5,000. Conversely, if what the transferor gives away is of special value to the transferee, this is also ignored as it is only the loss to the estate of the transferor which is considered. This principle may be of particular significance when disposing of shares in a company in which the transferor has a controlling interest either in his own right or where the related property provisions apply (see para **6.13**).

The grossing-up provisions

1.14 A consequence of the rule that the value transferred is the loss to the estate of the transferor is the 'grossing-up' provisions. These now only normally apply to lifetime chargeable transfers. If a transferor makes a transfer of value to a company of, say, £80,000 and pays the tax on that figure, then the loss to his estate will be not only the original gift but also the tax which he has paid which will itself in turn be taxed. This is considered in greater detail at para **3.13**. However, if the transferee in these circumstances bears the tax, then there is no necessity for grossing-up. Similarly, on a death, as the tax is deducted from the estate before distribution, there is no necessity for grossing-up. In the case of potentially exempt transfers made within seven years of death which subsequently become chargeable to tax, then the tax payable thereon is the responsibility of the transferee and, assuming it is met by him, there is no necessity for the grossing-up provisions to apply.

Consideration set-off

1.15   As it is the net loss to the estate of the transferor which is chargeable, if any consideration is given in return this will automatically be taken into account. So, for example, if property is sold at an under value, then it is only the amount of the under-value which represents the loss to the estate.

Interest-free loans

1.16   Originally the net loss to the transferor's estate by reason of making an interest-free loan or allowing a person to use property without payment of commercial rent specifically gave rise to a charge. This no longer applies with effect from 6 April 1981. Whether such free use of money or assets is a transfer of value will now depend on the general provisions. In most cases it would tend to be covered by the annual exemption or the normal and reasonable expenditure exemption. However, if the loan is not repayable on demand but is made for a fixed period free of interest, it is probable that a loss to the transferor's estate can be quantified; the value of such a loan in the transferor's estate will have to be discounted. Furthermore, if the loan is precarious, such as if the borrower is unable or unlikely to repay the loan, again it may amount to a transfer of value.

The position of guarantors

1.17   If there is no loss to the estate of the transferor, then there will be no transfer of value until such time as loss is suffered. If one person guarantees another's overdraft, there is no reduction in the value of the guarantor's until such time as the guarantee is called in and paid.

Persons domiciled outside the UK (s 6)

1.18   For the purposes of inheritance tax, the estate of a person does not include excluded property. This is defined as property situated outside the UK if the person beneficially entitled to it is an individual domiciled outside the UK. For this purpose the UK includes the mainland and Northern Ireland but excludes the Channel Islands and the Isle of Man.

Extended meaning of domicile

1.19   These provisions refer to domicile and not ordinary residence, which is the test for income tax purposes. If a person is domiciled in the UK under the general law, then he will be so domiciled for the purposes of inheritance tax. In addition, however, s 267 extends the meaning of 'domicile' for the purpose of this tax and a person will be deemed to be domiciled in the UK if *either*:

(a) he has been domiciled in the UK at any time within three years immediately preceding the transfer (this does not apply to a person who has not been domiciled in the UK at any time since 9 December 1974); *or*

(b) he was resident in the UK for not less than 17 of the 20 years of assessment ending with the year of assessment in which the transfer took place (this does not apply to a person who has not been resident in the UK since 9 December 1974).

The definition of residence is the same for income tax purposes except the fact that a person has a dwelling-house available for his use in the UK is disregarded for this purpose.

1.20 A person who is neither domiciled nor no longer resident in the UK under the general law, even though he may be treated as a person domiciled in the UK under the above provisions, can make a transfer of certain specified Government stocks which will be exempt from inheritance tax and include a wide range of Treasury, Funding and Exchequer stocks and War Loan (s 6(3)).

1.21 There is a further provision that if a person is domiciled in the Channel Islands or the Isle of Man, then certain other Government stocks are also excluded property and these consist of war savings certificates, national savings certificates, premium savings bonds, deposits with National Savings Bank or or a trustee savings bank and certified contractual savings schemes.

Reversionary interests (s 48)

1.22 A reversionary interest is an interest under a settlement which has not yet fallen into possession. So if property is settled on A for life with the remainder to B, then if B dies or disposes of his interest during A's lifetime, B's interest in remainder is excluded property and there is no charge to tax as there has been no change of any interest in possession in the trust fund. This is in contrast to the estate duty provisions which charged such interests but enabled an election to be made as to when the interest should be valued and the tax paid (see para **0.02**(2)).

Limitations

1.23 Under inheritance tax, reversionary interests are normally excluded property. However, to prevent exploitation of this immunity, it is provided in s 48 that a reversionary interest is not excluded property if:

(a) it has at any time been acquired (whether by the person entitled to it or by a person previously entitled to it) for a consideration in money or money's worth; or

(b) it is one to which either the settlor or his spouse is or has been beneficially entitled; or

(c) it is an interest expectant on the determination of a lease for life or lives granted for less than full consideration in money or money's worth.

However, a reversionary interest will always be excluded property if it is itself situated outside the UK and is either beneficially owned by an individual domiciled outside the UK or is itself settled property comprised in a settlement made by a settlor domiciled outside the UK when he made the settlement.

Dispositions by associated operations (s 268)

1.24 In determining whether a person has made a disposition resulting in a loss to his estate account has to be taken of any 'associated operations'.

Definition

1.25 Associated operations are defined as meaning any two or more operations of any kind, being:

(a) operations which affect the same property, or one which affects some property and the other or others of which affect a property which represents, whether directly or indirectly, that property;

(b) any two operations of which one is effected with reference to the other, or with a view to enabling the other to be effected or facilitating its being effected, or any further operation having like relation to any of those two,

whether those operations are effected by the same person or different persons and whether or not they are simultaneous.

Operation includes an omission

1.26 For this purpose an operation includes an omission. An operation effected after 26 March 1974 is not associated with one effected earlier.

Illustration of application of the rule

1.27   The purpose of these provisions is to prevent a transferor making a series of operations which taken individually would not amount to transfers of value but which taken together result in a loss to the transferor's estate.

EXAMPLE
A father, who has made no previous gifts, wishes to transfer £12,000 to his son. He does so by giving £6,000 to his son and £6,000 to his wife who then passes it on to the son. None of the individual payments would be chargeable. The gift by the father to the son is within the annual exemption, the gift by the spouse is exempt and the gift by the mother to the son is within the exemption. However, the overall effect of these three operations is treated as a disposition of £12,000 by the father to the son.

Operations involving spouses

1.28   However, the Inland Revenue do not in practice invoke the associated operations rule in dispositions between spouses unless it is blatant. So if, in the last example, the wife had no funds of her own and immediately made over the gift to the son or she simply endorsed her husband's cheque in favour of the son, it would be treated as blatant. It also appears that the Inland Revenue do not at the moment invoke the principle of *Furniss v Dawson* (see para **11.35**) in this connection.

The granting of a lease

1.29   This provision is often of particular relevance when letting property which is the subject of protection of tenure.

EXAMPLE
In 1986, a father owning a farm worth £1,000,000 lets it to his son at a full commercial rent. The son will be a protected tenant under the Agricultural Holdings Acts legislation and as such the value of the freehold reversion may well be reduced to half the vacant possession value.

In 1987, the father sells his son the freehold reversion at the commercial market price for agricultural propery subject to a tenancy at £500,000.

The net result is that the father will be deemed to have made a disposition to his son of the overall loss to his estate from these operations, namely £1,000,000.

1.30 However, s 268(2) expressly provides that the granting of a lease for full consideration in money or money's worth shall not be taken to be associated with any operation effected more than three years after the grant. Further, no operation effected on or after 27 March 1974 shall be associated with any operation effected before that date. If, therefore, in the above illustration the father had allowed three years to elapse before selling the freehold reversion, then the operations would not be associated and he could safely sell the property to his son at the tenanted price.

Agricultural tenancies (s 16(1))
1.31 Prior to the FA 1981 it was sometimes argued by the Inland Revenue that the granting of the agricultural tenancy, although at a full market rental, was itself a transfer of value resulting in a loss to the transferor's estate of the difference between the vacant possession and the tenanted values. This particular ambiguity, resolved by the FA 1981, s 97(1), is now contained in s 61(1) which expressly provides that the grant of a tenancy of agricultural property in the UK, the Channel Islands or Isle of Man for use for agricultural purposes is not a transfer of value by the grantor if he makes it in full consideration of money or money's worth. This provision expressly applies to agricultural property, so by implication it may not extend to other types of tenancies, such as those protected under the Rent Acts or business tenancies.

Death as an associated operation

1.32 It would seem that death itself is not an associated operation. However, it is arguable that a testamentary disposition which takes effect on death may, in certain circumstances, be treated as an operation. In *Bambridge v IRC*, a case involving income tax, the definition of an associated operation contained in the FA 1936, s 18(2), which was there defined as 'an operation of any kind effected by a person in relation to any of the assets transferred' had to be considered. It was accepted by the Crown that death was not an associated operation, but it was held by the House of Lords that the definition under that section was wide enough to include, prima facie, the making of a will which takes effect on death. The purpose of making the will was to put into effect at some future date the provisions of the will itself and therefore the making of the will was itself an associated operation. While at first sight this should not extend to an intestacy, as an operation can include an omission, it would seem it could be extended to such a situation.

The last operation constitutes the date of the transfer

1.33   Where the associated operations provisions apply, the transfer of value is deemed to be made at the date of the last operation. This could be important in a number of respects:

(1)   If the transfer is a lifetime chargeable transfer, the loss to the transferor's estate will be established at that time, and may be significantly higher than when the first operation took place.

(2)   For the purpose of cumulation, the seven-year cumulation period will not start to run until the last operation has been effected.

(3)   For the purpose of ascertaining whether a potentially exempt transfer becomes an exempt transfer, the seven-year period will not start to run until the final operation.

(4)   The date of the last operation will be relevant in calculating the tapered relief applying to lifetime chargeable transfers and potentially exempt transfers made within the seven years before the date of death.

(5)   In respect of lifetime transfers of property qualifying for business property relief, the transferee must retain ownership of the property for seven years prior to the transferor's death (see para **7.12**). The seven-year period will not start to run until the date of the last operation.

(6)   Similarly in respect of lifetime transfers of property qualifying for agricultural property relief, the transferee must retain ownership of the property for seven years prior to the transferor's death (see para **7.59**). Again the seven-year period does not start to run until the date of the last operation.

DISPOSITIONS THAT ARE NOT TRANSFERS OF VALUE (ss 10–17)

1.34   The 1984 Act provides that certain dispositions are not deemed to be transfers of value. This category of dispositions should be distinguished from the exemptions under Chapter 5 which are transfers of value, but are exempt from the charge of tax.

Dispositions not intended to confer gratuitous benefit (s 10)

1.35   Inheritance tax is intended to be a tax on gratuitous transfers of value. If full consideration is given for the transfer, then there is no loss to the transferor's estate and therefore no transfer of value. However, in many cases there will not always be an exact equivalence of consideration. To resolve these situations, s 10 provides that certain cases are not to be treated as transfers of value.

Definition

1.36   A disposition is stated not to be a transfer of value if the transferor shows:

(a)   that it was not intended, and was not made in a transaction intended, to confer any gratuitous benefit on any person; *and*

(b)   either (i)   that it was made in a transaction at arm's length between persons not connected with each other, *or*

(ii)   that it was such that might be expected to be made in a transaction at arm's length between persons not connected with each other.

No gratuitous benefit
1.37   The burden is on the transferor to show that there was no intention to confer a gratuitous benefit. Further, the intention will be judged according to the normal presumption that a person is presumed to intend the natural and probable consequences of his acts (or omissions), so that if the transaction is at an under value such intention will be prima facie presumed.

Illustration
1.38   The operation of s 10 can be illustrated with an example.

EXAMPLE
A father holds a 75% shareholding in a company and the 25% balance is held by an unconnected person. The father then gives 30% of the shares in the company to his son. The loss to the father's estate is greater than the market value of a 30% shareholding in the company as he has lost control of the company and power to pass a special resolution. It will therefore be a chargeable transfer to the full extent of that loss.

Alternatively, if the son had paid the father the full market value of a 30% share holding in the company, while there would still be a loss to the transferor's estate, if it can be brought within this section, then it will not be a transfer of value.

On the other hand, if it does not fall within the section, the *full* loss to the transferor's estate will be the transfer of value. This may arise if, for example, the son had paid a price slightly lower than the market value of a 30% minority holding.

A series of transactions included

1.39 The word 'transaction' under s 10 is defined as including a series of transactions and any associated operations. This is an anti-avoidance device to provide for the situation where, for example, an asset is transferred in stages, full consideration being given for each individual transaction but the overall effect of which would not be expected to be a transaction which would be made at arm's length between unconnected persons.

Connected persons

1.40 Connected persons are defined by reference to s 270. A person is connected with his relatives, which are defined as his spouse, brother, sister, ancestor, lineal descendant, uncle, aunt, nephew and niece, and with the spouse of such persons. Further, a trustee of a settlement in that capacity is connected with the settlor, with any person connected with the settlor and with a body corporate treated as a settlor. A partner is connected not only with his partners but also with relatives, as defined, of his individual partners, unless the transfer is in relation to bona fide commercial disposals of partnership assets. There are also provisions with regard to persons controlling companies.

Unquoted shares

1.41 These provisions do not apply to a sale of shares or debentures not quoted on a recognised Stock Exchange unless it is shown that the sale was at a price freely negotiated at the time of the sale or at a price such as might be expected to be freely negotiated at the time of the sale.

Dispositions for maintenance of family (s 11)

1.42 It is provided that certain dispositions for the maintenance of one's family are not transfers of value:

(i)   if it is made by one party to the marriage in favour of the other and is for the maintenance of the other party. In view of the spouse exemption, this would normally only be of any relevance if the transferor is, but the transferee is not, domiciled in the UK; or

(ii)   if the disposition is in favour of a child of either party to the marriage and is for the maintenance, education or training of the child for a period ending not later than the year in which he attains the age of 18 or, after attaining that age, ceases to undergo full-time education or training.

1.43   The section contains various other provisions providing that a disposition is also not a transfer of value if made in favour of a child who is under the age of 18 or undergoing full-time education or training but has for a substantial time been in the care of the person making the disposition.

1.44   Nor is a disposition a transfer of value if it is made in favour of a dependent relative of the person making the disposition and is a reasonable provision for his care or maintenance.

Other miscellaneous provisions (ss 12–15)

1.45   It is provided by s 12 that a disposition which is allowable in computing the transferor's profits or gains for income tax or corporation tax is not a transfer of value. The same section covers dispositions for retirement benefit schemes and occupations of a dwelling at a subsidised rent or rent free.

1.46   There is a provision in s 13 to provide that certain dispositions by close companies for the benefit of employees are not transfers of value.

1.47   Sections 14 and 15 provide that waiver of remuneration or waiver of dividends does not constitute a transfer of value.

CHAPTER 2

Potentially exempt transfers and gifts with reservation

Introduction

2.01 The objective of this chapter is to consider and illustrate the operation of two of the major new provisions contained in the FA 1986. A potentially exempt transfer is a new concept, whereas the provisions relating to gifts with reservation are a revival of the estate duty rule.

2.02 The other changes effected by the FA 1986 referred to in this Guide may be found by referring to Appendix A.

POTENTIALLY EXEMPT TRANSFERS

2.03 The FA 1986 introduced a new category of transfer of value defined as a 'potentially exempt transfer'. This was effected by inserting a new s 3(A) in the 1984 Act (by Sch 19, para 1 of the FA 1986). These transfers do not attract a lifetime charge to tax, nor a charge to death if the transferor survives the gift by seven years, provided he has not reserved any benefit from the gift.

Definition (s 3(A), inserted by the FA 1986, Sch 19, para 1)

2.04 A potentially exempt transfer is one:

(a) which is made by an individual on or after 18 March 1986; *and*
(b) which would otherwise be a chargeable transfer, *and*
(c) which is a gift to another individual or a gift into an accumulation and maintenance trust or a disabled trust.

A transfer made by an individual

2.05 To constitute a potentially exempt transfer, the transfer must be made by an individual. While a company can make a transfer of value, it cannot make a chargeable transfer of value as this can only be made by an individual (s 2(1)). However, in the case of a close company, the loss suffered by the company will be apportioned between the participants (see para **3.16**). Such a transfer will therefore continue to be an occasion of charge under the existing rules at the time it is made. Further, where by virtue of s 98 there is a deemed disposition by the participants involving alterations in the capital of a close company (see para **3.22**) this is treated effectively as a lifetime chargeable transfer apportioned between the participants. (S 93(3), inserted by the FA·1986, Sch 19, para 20).

A transfer to an individual or a favoured trust

2.06 There is the final requirement that the transfer must be to another individual or a gift into an accumulation and maintenance trust or a disabled trust. A gift to a company or a gift into any other form of trust other than those specified would not constitute a potentially exempt transfer. The definition of an accumulation and maintenance trust and a disabled trust is the same as that required for establishing these trusts under ss 71 and 89 of the 1984 Act and which are considered in Chapter 8.

Transfers prior to 18 March 1986 unaffected

2.07 If the transfer is made before 18 March 1986, it will be governed by the previous rules applying on the date of transfer. This could be of importance if the tax on the transfer were less than it would have been if made after 17 March 1986. This would normally arise where the death occurs between the third and fifth year from the date of the transfer where under the new provisions more than half the death rate would be payable. This is specifically covered in the transitional provisions (FA 1986, Sch 19, para 40(1)) which provide that nothing in the FA 1986 shall affect the tax chargeable on a transfer occurring before 18 March 1986.

The usual exemptions apply

2.08 If the transfer is not one which would otherwise be chargeable, then it is not a potentially exempt transfer. The recognised exceptions applying to other transfers also apply to potentially exempt transfers, such as, for example, the spouse exemption or the annual £3,000 exemption to the extent of that exemption (subject to the modification mentioned in para **2.13**).

Consequences

An exempt transfer after seven years

2.09 Once a transfer of value is established as a potentially exempt transfer, then it becomes an exempt transfer once the transferor has survived the gift by seven years (s 3A(4), inserted by the FA 1986, Sch 19, para 1).

Converted into a chargeable transfer within seven years

2.10 In the event of the transferor dying within the seven years, then it becomes a chargeable transfer (s 3A(4)).

Cumulation

2.11 The effect of this is that the transfer will be cumulated with any other chargeable transfers made within seven years of the transferor's death and with the transferor's estate, and, unless the transfer falls within the nil band, will be taxed at that stage.

Rate of tax applying at date of death

2.12 The tax will be calculated on the value of the transfer at the time it was made, but the rate of tax will be that applicable at the date of the transferor's death and not at the date of the transfer (s 1(A), inserted by the FA 1986, Sch 19, para 3(2)).

Application of the annual exemption

2.13 For the purpose of calculating tax, if the transferor dies within the seven years so that the transfer becomes a chargeable transfer, then the transfer will be deemed to have been made at the date at which it is made. To this there is the express exception (s 19(3A), inserted by the FA 1986, Sch 19, para 5) that for the purpose of the annual exemption, the transfer is deemed to have been made after any other transfers of value in that tax year which are not potentially exempt and which would be able to absorb the annual relief before the potentially exempt transfer which has subsequently become chargeable.

EXAMPLE
In July 1986, a father who has made no previous transfers, gives £80,000 to his son. In December 1986, he transfers £21,000 into an interest in possession trust. The father dies in January 1987.

For the purpose only of the annual relief, the tax on the potentially exempt transfer of £80,000 made in July will be deemed to have been made after the lifetime chargeable transfer of £21,000 made in December. The tax payable on the first gift will therefore be based on £80,000, viz £2,700. The second gift for the purpose only of applying the annual exemption, will be deemed to have been made first, so attracting £6,000 exemption (including the previous year's carry forward) and will therefore bear tax on £15,000 on the band appropriate between £80,000 and £95,000, viz £4,500. It is, of course, only necessary to use the annual exemption in the case of a potentially exempt transfer if the transferor fails to survive the transfer by seven years.

Payment of tax

2.14 The tax, which is the primary liability of the transferee, does not fall due until six months after the end of the month in which the donor's death occurs (see para **9.25**). It should be noted, however, that the option to pay by instalments on qualifying property is lost if a property is disposed of by the transferee before the date of the donor's death (see para **9.33**).

Tapered relief

2.15 The tax payable will be at the full rate if the transferor has died within three years of making the transfer. If the transferor has survived the gift by more than three years, then the amount of tax payable is reduced by 20% on each of the successive years as follows (s 7(4), inserted by the FA 1986, Sch 19, para 2(4)).

Years between gift and death	*Percentage of tax payable*
0 — 3	100%
3 — 4	80%
4 — 5	60%
5 — 6	40%
6 — 7	20%

2.16 It will therefore be appreciated that while the amount of tax payable is reduced by the appropriate percentage, it does not reduce the value of the gift for the purpose of cumulation with any other chargeable transfers and the estate, as illustrated in para **2.19**.

Valuation relief where assets sold before death (s 131)

2.17 Where following the death of the transferee within seven years of the transfer, any tax which becomes payable in respect of a

25

potentially exempt transfer is generally calculated by reference to the value actually transferred. However, relief is given by s 131 if the property transferred has been continuously held by the transferee or his spouse when there has been a qualifying sale. The detailed considerations which are required to qualify for this relief are set out in para **4.06**.

Differences from previous estate duty rules

2.18   These provisions therefore differ from those which used to apply to estate duty in two respects:

(1)   tax is calculated on the value of the gift at the date it is made, whereas in the case of estate duty it was calculated in accordance with the value of the gift at the date of death;

(2)   while the transfers are cumulated with the estate and any other chargeable transfers for the purpose of ascertaining the tax payable on any subsequent chargeable transfers or on death, they are not aggregated with the estate, as was the case with estate duty, for the purpose of ascertaining an 'estate rate' by which the total duty payable was rateably apportioned between the gifts and the estate. The full marginal rate of tax therefore now falls on the estate, as in the case of other lifetime transfers.

Operational example

2.19   The operation of these provisions can best be illustrated with an example:

EXAMPLE
In May 1986 a father, who has no carry forward of the annual relief, makes a gift to his son of his town house, at that time worth £83,000. In May 1987, he makes a gift of his country cottage to his daughter worth £53,000.

In June 1991 he dies leaving his estate worth £50,000 to his grandson. At that time the value of the house had risen to £100,000 and of the cottage to £70,000. The tax will be calculated as follows:

The gift to the son is valued at the date it is made and after allowing for the annual exemption the chargeable transfer is £80,000. This would be charged to tax on the tax table applicable at the date of death, so with indexation by 1991 the gift would almost certainly fall within the nil band. However, if tax is payable, it will be at 40% as the death occurred between the fifth and sixth year.

The gift to the daughter will be taxed at the rate of tax applicable at the date of death between £80,000 and £130,000 (allowing for annual relief). The tax actually payable will be reduced to 60% as the death occurred between the fourth and fifth year.

On his death, the father's estate will be taxed at the marginal rate of tax applicable between £130,000 and £180,000.

Reassessment of transfers

2.20 A potentially exempt transfer which proves to be a chargeable transfer is deemed to be made on the day it was actually made (apart from the special provision relating to the allocation of the annual relief, on which see para **2.13**). This may necessitate a reassessment of all subsequent chargeable transfers.

EXAMPLE

A father, who has made no previous transfers, makes a gift of £75,000 to his son in July 1986. In August, he transfers £60,000 into an interest in possession trust. The father dies in December 1986.

When the gift into trust is made in August, no tax would be payable as it falls within the nil band, there having been no earlier chargeable transfers. However, on the father's death, tax will have to be re-assessed in the order in which the gifts were made. The gift in July would attract tax of £1,200 (viz 30% of £4,000, the later gift not being a potentially exempt transfer, would utilise the annual exemption first). The gift in August would now have to be reassessed on the basis that there had been a previous chargeable transfer of £75,000; after utilising the previous and current years annual exemptions, the chargeable transfer would be £54,000 taxed between the bands of £75,000 and £129,000, resulting in tax of £17,900.

Term life assurance

2.21 The potential tax liability arising from such reassessments, which may be unexpectedly compounded if an earlier transfer loses its business property relief or agricultural property relief (see paras **7.12** and **7.59** respectively), would certainly justify advising term life assurance in such circumstances.

Discharge certificate

2.22 Delay in resolving the problems arising from reassessments has been anticipated, as it is specifically provided that in respect of a potentially exempt transfer an application for a certificate of discharge may not be normally made until two years after the date of death of the transferor (s 239(2A) inserted by the FA 1986, Sch 19, para 35)!

GIFTS WITH RESERVATION (FA 1986, s 102)

2.23 This principle of estate duty has been reintroduced into inheritance tax. If a transferor makes a gift of a property which under these provisions is deemed to be property subject to a reservation in favour of the transferor, then for tax purposes he is not deemed to have made a gift of it until such time as the benefit of the reservation ceases or on death if it still continues until then.

2.24 These provisions apply to *all* gifts made after 17 March 1986, not merely potentially exempt transfers.

Definition (FA 1986, s 102(1))

2.25 Where a person disposes of any property by way of gift after 17 March 1986 and either:

(a)   possession and enjoyment of the property is not bona fide assumed by the donee seven or more years before the date of death of the donor (or the date of the gift if later); or

(b)   at any time within seven years before the date of death of the donor (or the date of the gift if later) the property is not enjoyed to the entire exclusion, or virtually to the entire exclusion, of the donor and of any benefit to him by contract or otherwise,

the property is referred to as property subject to a reservation.

2.26 Property treated as falling within this definition is discussed in detail below, but first the consequences are to be considered.

Consequences

Reservation ceasing in lifetime

2.27 If the property ceases to be property subject to a reservation before the donor's death, then at the moment the reservation ceases the donor is deemed to have disposed of the property by making a potentially exempt transfer. In this case the value will be established at that time and the other provisions relating to potentially exempt transfers will come into operation.

Reservation ceasing on death

2.28 However, if the property continues to be subject to a reservation up to the date of the donor's death, then it is treated as property to which the donor was beneficially entitled immediately before his death. This being so, it will be aggregated, not merely cumulated with the donor's estate. This has four implications:

(1) The gift will not qualify for the annual exemption or the normal expenditure exemption (see para **2.32**).
(2) The property will be valued for tax purposes as at the date of the death of the donor and not at the date of the gift.
(3) The rate of tax will be that applying at date of death.
(4) The property will be aggregated, not merely cumulated, with the estate of the deceased. The effect of this is that the gifted property and the estate will be added together for the purposes of ascertaining the total tax and the tax then apportioned rateably between the gift and the estate as it used to be for estate duty purposes.

Aggregation with the estate

2.29 The effect of these provisions appear to produce the strange result that if a gifted property ceases to be property subject to a reservation at any time before death, while it will be cumulated with any other gifts and with the estate of the donor, it will not be aggregated with it, which means that the marginal rate of tax will be borne by the estate. On the other hand, if the property continues to be subject to a reservation on death, it is treated as property to which the donor was beneficially entitled immediately before his death and as such will be aggregated with the estate and the tax rateably apportioned between the donee and the estate.

2.30 These implications can be illustrated with an example:

EXAMPLE
In July 1986 a father, who has made no previous transfers, makes a gift of his home, at that time worth £80,000, to his son, but the father continues to live in the property up to the date of his death in July 1991, when he dies leaving an estate of £100,000 to his daughter.

On the father's death the value of his house is £100,000. As he has continued to live in the house until the date of his death, then it will be deemed to be property subject to a reservation and as such treated as property to which he is beneficially entitled immediately before his death. The £100,000 will therefore be added to the value of his estate of £100,000 making a total of £200,000. The tax payable on £200,000 at the date of death will be calculated and this will be borne equally between the son and the daughter. On the current Table the tax would be £49,300, that is £24,650 each.

If the gift of the house had not been of property subject to a reservation, tax would have been payable by the son on £74,000 (using the previous and current years' annual exemptions) based on the table applying at the date of the father's death, so with indexation to 1991 would probably escape tax. However, on the current Table this would be £900 at 80% (death in the fourth year) namely £720. The tax on the estate would be at the marginal rate applying between £74,000 and £174,000; again using the current Table this would amount at a tax of £36,700 being paid by the daughter.

Family feuds

2.31 In this example one could envisage the daughter endeavouring to establish that the gift to the son was subject to a reservation so reducing her tax liability, while the son would be endeavouring to establish that it was not so subject by virtue of the relief given in the FA 1986, Sch 20, para 6(1)(b) (see para **2.49**). The Inland Revenue would simply sit on the sidelines! One would also normally envisage some compromise being reached between the personal representatives and the lifetime transferee, but if the beneficiaries under the estate are minors, such compromise would not be possible without an application to the court. If the personal representatives failed to endeavour to establish such a claim that the lifetime gift was still subject to a reservation, they could subsequently be liable for having failed to reduce the tax on the free estate!

Exemptions

2.32 Notwithstanding that property subject to a reservation ceasing on death is treated as property to which the deceased was beneficially entitled immediately before his death, it is expressly provided by the FA 1986, s 102(5) that all the exemptions contained in Chapter 5 apply to such gifts with the exception of the annual exemption and the normal expenditure out of income exemption which cannot be claimed in respect of such gifts.

Liability and payment

2.33 The donee is primarily liable for tax on property subject to a reservation (FA 1986, Sch 19, paras 28(3), 29) and the tax falls due six months after the end of the month in which the donor's death occurs (see para **9.25**).

Post-death variations excluded

2.34 Where property is subject to a reservation immediately before the donor's death it is treated as property to which he was beneficially entitled immediately before his death. However, it is specifically provided that such property cannot be varied within two years of the date of death notwithstanding that it is deemed to form part of his estate for tax purposes (FA 1986, Sch 19, para 24).

Capital gains tax implications

2.35 A gift of property subject to a reservation will be treated as a disposal made by the donor at the date of the gift. While an election may be made for hold-over relief, there will be no uplift in the value of the property on death. Therefore the donee of property subject to a reservation has the worst of both worlds: he shares the marginal rate of tax based on the value of the property at the date of death, but with no uplift in value to reduce potential future capital gains tax liability.

FURTHER CONSIDERATION OF THE DEFINITION
(FA 1986, s 102)

2.36 The wording used in s 102(1) is substantially the same wording, in a more modern form, as that applying to estate duty under the Customs and Inland Revenue Act 1889, s 11(1), except for the insertion of the words 'or virtually to the entire exclusion'. These additional words would perhaps exclude the occasional loan of a gifted car, or an occasional visit to gifted property, being treated as a reservation of benefit. Further, there are two limited express exceptions where full consideration is given (see para **2.47**) or where provision is made for a donor who has become infirm (para **2.49**).

Possession and enjoyment assumed by the donee (FA 1986, s 102(1)(a))

2.37 The gifted property will be regarded as property subject to a reservation if the possession and enjoyment of the gifted property is not bona fide assumed by the donee.

Property must be vested in donee

2.38   This requirement means that the beneficial interest in the property must have been effectively vested in the donee. This will be a matter for the general law as, in the absence of consideration, the donor must have vested his title in the donee before the gift becomes complete. If there is an imperfect gift, then this requirement will not be satisfied. This could arise because the donor has not used the correct method for transferring the title. So for example, in the case of the transfer of a legal estate in land, he must use a deed and in the case of a disposition of a subsisting equitable interest in property of whatever kind it must be effected in writing (LPA 1925, s 53(1)(c)); *Grey v IRC*. Likewise if the donor gives the donee his own cheque which is only a revocable order to his bankers, then the gift is not complete until such time as the cheque is cleared; this is in contrast to the donor endorsing over to the donee a cheque drawn in the donor's favour.

Substitutions and accretions

2.39   The original estate duty provisions contained in s 11(1) of the Customs and Inland Revenue Act 1889 required that the enjoyment of the donee should be assumed 'and thenceforward retained'. These words are not included in the FA 1986, s 102, but Sch 20, para 2, contains provisions providing that where the donee has disposed of the gifted property by sale, gift (except to the donor) or on a beneficiary's death, he is required to have possession and enjoyment of any property substituted for the original gifted property. Identification of the gifted property is also necessary for the purpose of its valuation on death.

Exclusion of the donor (FA 1986, s 102(1)(b))

2.40   The gifted property will also be regarded as property subject to a reservation if at any time from the date of the gift and within the seven years before the date of death the property is not enjoyed to the entire exclusion, or virtually to the entire exclusion, of the donor and of any benefit to him by contract or otherwise.

2.41   This wording essentially follows the estate duty provisions apart from the addition of the words 'or virtually to the entire exclusion'. In *Chick v Stamp Duties Comrs* it was considered that this requirement constituted two distinct limbs. The possession and enjoyment must be:

(a)   to the entire exclusion, or virtually to the entire exclusion, of the donor; *and*

(b)   to the entire exclusion, or virtually to the entire exclusion, of any benefit to him by contract or otherwise.

The entire exclusion of the donor

2.42   The first limb, requiring the entire exclusion, or virtually the entire exclusion, of the donor necessitates exclusion not only in law but also in fact, and the donor will not be entirely excluded even if he gives full consideration for such interest as he may have, (subject as mentioned below at para **2.47**). It is a clear reservation of benefit if the donor imposes a legal obligation on the donee to pay the income arising from the gifted property to the donor during his life. However, if there is a mere understanding that the donee will pay back the income from the property to the donor, then the donor is not regarded as having been entirely excluded. Even if there was no such understanding at the time of the gift, if the donor subsequently derives a benefit from the gifted property within the seven years before the date of death, this will make the property subject to a reservation.

2.43   This is illustrated by the decision of *Stamp Duty Comr of New South Wales v Permanent Trustee Co of New South Wales*. In that case the deceased in 1924 had made a settlement for the benefit of his infant daughter contingently on her attaining the age of 30 years. The terms of the settlement ensured that the donor was wholly excluded from any benefit under it. In 1938, shortly before the daughter attained the specified age, the deceased came to an arrangement with his daughter to borrow the income from the trust fund to enable him to reduce his own overdraft. On the deceased's death within the statutory period (then five years) after he had borrowed the funds, it was held the gift which he had made in 1924 was subject to estate duty.

Enjoyment during the critical 'relevant period'

2.44   Under the estate duty provisions, therefore, even if the gift had not been enjoyed by the donor for more than the statutory period but subsequently he enjoyed it within the statutory period, then he had not been entirely excluded from the property.

2.45   The same applies under inheritance tax in respect of any property which is subject to a reservation, as the donor must be excluded from the property for the 'relevant period' which is defined as the period ending on the date of the donor's death and beginning seven years before that date or, if it is later, on the date of the gift.

Chick v Stamp Duties Comrs

2.46 A leading case illustrating the principle that a donor is not excluded from the subject matter of the gift, even if he gives the donee full consideration for that interest, is *Chick v Stamp Duties Comrs* (above). A father in 1934 made an absolute gift of grazing land to his son. A year later the son brought the grazing land into a farming partnership with his father and his brother. It was accepted that full consideration was given by all the partners under the terms of the partnership agreement, but it was nevertheless held that, on the father's death in 1952, his son had not retained possession and enjoyment of the gifted property to the donor's entire exclusion, so duty was payable in respect of the gift which had been made in 1934.

Relaxation if enjoyed for full consideration in money or money's worth

2.47 The rigour of the principle established in *Chick's* case was modified by the FA 1959, s 35(2) in relation to gifts of land and chattels. This provision has also been reintroduced (FA 1986, Sch 20, para 6(1a)). It is provided that, in relation to gifts of land or chattels, actual occupation of the land, or actual enjoyment of an incorporeal right over the land, or actual possession of the chattels by the donor, shall be disregarded if it is for full consideration in money or money's worth. This relaxation would enable the donor to make a gift of his house to a donee, but continue to live there provided he pays a full market rent to the donee; but if he pays only slightly less than the full market rent, the gift will be treated as subject to reservation. Further, full consideration paid to the donee for some interest in gifted property taken back by the donor will not fall within this relaxation unless the property is land or chattels and the nature of the interest taken by the donor is actual occupation thereof or enjoyment of an incorporeal right over the land.

2.48 Particular care must therefore be taken if a donor continues to occupy gifted property as a tenant, for example as a partner. If the tenancy from the donee back to the partnership is even slightly less than a full market rental, then the property will be subject to a reservation to the donor. Even if the rent is initially at a full market rental, but is not reviewed on a commercial basis, then the property may subsequently be regarded as subject to a reservation.

Relaxation where the donor has become infirm

2.49 A further relaxation, which did not apply to estate duty, is given (FA 1986, Sch 20, para 6(1)(b)). In the case of property which is an interest in land, any occupation by the donor of the whole or any part of the land shall be disregarded if—

(i) it results from a change in the circumstances of the donor since the time of the gift, being a change which was unforeseen at that time and was not brought about by the donor to receive the benefit of this provision; and

(ii) it occurs at a time when the donor has become unable to maintain himself through old age, infirmity or otherwise; and

(iii) it represents a reasonable provision by the donee for the care and maintenance of the donor; and

(iv) the donee is a relative of the donor or his spouse.

2.50 It will be seen that this concession only applies to an interest in *land* (so, for example, would not include furniture) and is intended to cover a situation where a donor relative through unforeseen changed circumstances has become unable to maintain himself and it would be reasonable to expect provision to be made by the donee. Provided the requirements are met it would seem that, for example, where a father has made a gift of some property to his son and then some years later in old age he is unable to maintain himself and is invited into the son's home, or perhaps into a 'granny' annexe so that his family can look after him, the concession will apply.

Joint tenancies

2.51 A particular danger arises where a donor gifts property into the names of a donee and himself as beneficial joint tenants. Since there is the possibility that the donor will survive the donee and thus reacquire the whole property by survivorship, the gift of the half share in the property will be treated as being subject to a reservation.

2.52 The same will not apply in the case of a tenancy in common provided that the donor does not receive more than his share of the income from the property.

Other joint assets

2.53 The same principle can also apply in the case of any other joint assets, such as joint bank accounts, which may pass to the donee by survivorship. This used to be a particular problem in the estate duty era when husbands would frequently vest their accounts in the names of their wife and themself and many years later the whole bank account would attract estate duty (at a time when gifts between spouses were not exempt).

Exclusion of the donor from all benefit by contract or otherwise

2.54   The second limb of the provisions requiring the exclusion of the donor is that he should be excluded not only from any benefit in the gifted property but he must also be excluded from all benefit by contract or otherwise. Therefore a collateral benefit, such as a separate covenant by the donee to pay the donor an annuity, even though not reserved out of the property given, would constitute a benefit to the donor. It is expressly provided that a benefit which the donor obtained by virtue of any associated operation (as defined in s 268 of the 1984 Act), of which the disposal by way of gift is one, shall be treated as a benefit to him by contract or otherwise (FA 1986, Sch 20, para 6(1)(c)).

Retention or reservation of benefit?

2.55   If the donor simply retains something which he has never given, then he is not regarded as having retained any benefit. This would apply, for example, if a father owns a house and an adjoining field and he gives the field to his son but reserves a right of way over the field for access to the highway: this will not be regarded as a reservation of benefit; he has simply not given that particular interest to his son as he has given the land excluding the easement.

Munro v Stamp Duty Comr

2.56   If the donor makes a gift of a certain interest in property, but retains other pre-existing interests in that property, again he does not reserve a benefit to himself. This was illustrated in *Munro v Stamp Duty Comr*. In that case a father owned freehold land on which he and his six children carried on the business of sheep farming in partnership. In 1913 he made a gift of the land to his children but he remained a partner in the business until his death in 1929. Estate duty was claimed on the land which he had given to his children in 1913 on the ground that he had not been excluded from all benefit, by reason of his retention of the interest which he had in the land as a partner in the business. It was held that the subject matter of the gift was not the entire property in the land, but his interest in the land subject to the rights of the partnership. It is only possible to distinguish this case from *Chick's* case above on the basis that in *Munro's* case the father's interest in the partnership was already in existence when he made the gift, whereas in *Chick's* case the father's interest was taken back out of the property which he had already given away.

Charging clause in trust deed

2.57   Care should be taken that there is no inadvertent benefit to the donor. As an example, if the donor is a trustee of a maintenance and accumulation trust made by him in his lifetime, if he is entitled to remuneration as a trustee under a power contained in a settlement, then the settlement would constitute a benefit to him even though he may have survived the settlement by seven years.

'Or otherwise'

2.58 The meaning of the words 'or otherwise' in the expression 'by contract or otherwise' has not been finally settled by the courts, although it had to be considered in *A-G v Seccombe*. In that case the donor had made a gift of his farm to his great nephew who lived with him in the farmhouse and had the year prior to the gift taken over the management of the farm. The donor continued to live in the farmhouse until his death nine years later and during that time was maintained by the donee who was then regarded as the head of the household. There was no enforceable agreement or any other under-standing between the parties that the donor should continue to live in and be maintained by the donee, although it is doubtful whether either party contemplated that the donor should be turned out of the farmhouse. It was held that the donee had assumed possession and enjoyment to the entire exclusion of the donor and of any benefit to him by contract or otherwise. It was said that the words 'or otherwise' must be construed as meaning some arrangement ejusdem generis with contract in the sense of some legally enforceable agreement.

2.59 The view expressed in the last case was adopted, obiter, by the Court of Appeal without argument on that point in the case of *A-G v St Aubyn*. However, this does seem somewhat surprising as if a benefit is actually taken this will bring it within the first limb whether or not there is a legally enforceable right.

2.60 One of the last decisions in this area before the abolition of estate duty was *Nichols v IRC*. In that case the Court of Appeal held that a gift of a freehold property subject to a condition that it would be leased back was regarded as a gift of the freehold subject to a reservation of benefit out of it, not a gift of a reversionary interest in the property leaving the donor with something which was not part of the subject matter of the gift.

Benefit by associated operations

2.61 It is further provided that the benefit which the donor obtains by virtue of any associated operations is treated as a benefit to him by contract or otherwise (FA 1986, Sch 20, para 6(1)(c)).

Omissions

2.62 These provisions relating to gifts with reservation refer to gifts rather than transfers of value so, for example, it is possible that an omission to exercise a right would probably not be construed as a gift.

Artificial debts (FA 1986, s 103)

2.63 The gift with reservation provisions cannot be avoided by artificially creating a debt to offset the value of the property in which the benefit is reserved. So, for example, if a father made a gift of his house to his son and then purchased it back at full market value, leaving the purchase price unpaid, the unpaid purchase price would not be an allowable deduction from his estate. For further consideration of such disallowable debts see para **6.39**.

Schemes for mitigating capital transfer tax curtailed

2.64 Any capital transfer tax scheme which involved any element of retention of benefit to the donor will now fall foul of the gift with reservation provisions. It is not intended to refer to specific schemes but rather to consider in general terms the broad class of schemes. No schemes effected before 18 March 1986 will be retrospectively affected.

Carving out or retention of benefit schemes

2.65 Some schemes for mitigating capital transfer tax operated on the principle that a transfer of value is the net loss to the transferor's estate. If the transferor first carved out or retained a benefit for himself before gifting the depleted asset, the loss to his estate was thereby reduced. Some such schemes may in any event have offended the associated operations rules, but will now certainly fall foul of the gift with reservation provisions.

Insurance schemes

2.66 Certain insurance schemes had a common theme that the donor put money into an insurance contract or into trust (or sometimes both) on terms that ensured that it passed directly to his beneficiaries on his death, but allowed him to benefit from the arrangement until that time. Such arrangements have been variously known as Pure Endowment-Term Assurance schemes, Discounted Gift Schemes and Inheritance Trusts. These will now all fall foul of the gifts with reservation provisions if effected after 17 March 1986.

Date effected

2.67 Whether such a scheme has been effected before 18 March 1986 is a matter of the general law of contract. If an offer has been accepted by an insurer, which on the contract would be at the time of the posting of the letter of acceptance, it will be effective provided this was done before midnight 17 March 1986.

Other policies on life of donor or his spouse

2.68 Any insurance scheme involving policies on the life of a donor or his spouse or on their joint lives will fall foul of the gift with reservation provisions if any benefits may accrue to the donor or his spouse (FA 1986, Sch 20, para 7).

Premiums on existing policies

2.69 The continued payment of regular premiums on an insurance policy made before 18 March 1986 and not subsequently varied will not normally offend these provisions (FA 1986, s 102(6)).

Use of annual gift exemption

2.70 An intending donor or his spouse may be unable to make cash gifts enabling them to utilise the annual exemption. Instead the donor may transfer a share in an asset each year up to the amount of the annual exemption. In any event, care had to be taken with such schemes as the loss to the transferor's estate may exceed the benefit transferred, such as the gift of a single share may result in the donor's loss of control of a company, or a gift of a parcel of land may substantially reduce the value of the property retained. Any such scheme where the donor retains a benefit, such as where he transfers a parcel of land but continues to occupy it or enjoy the income from it, will now fall foul of the gift with reservation provisions.

Transfers within capital accounts

2.71 It is not an uncommon practice for a donor partner to give instructions each year that his capital account should be debited with the amount of the annual exemption and the capital account of the donee be credited with a similar sum. It is arguable that such a procedure would offend the associated operations provisions, but in practice rarely is this point taken. However, if this procedure is now adopted, it is arguable that the objective of transferring the capital from the donor to the donee is nullified by the gift with reservation provisions as the donor partner continues to benefit from the use of the capital within the partnership.

Scrutinise all gifts

2.72   Every form of intended gift should now be carefully scrutinised to ensure that any arrangements made do not fall foul of the gift with reservation provisions. In particular it should be borne in mind that the benefit reserved does not have to have any relationship to the value of the gifted property; a small benefit reserved out of substantial gifted assets will still make the whole gift fall foul of these provisions.

Regulations for avoiding double charges (FA 1986, s 104).

2.73   Under the new rules there are ample opportunities for double charges and the possible categories in respect of which regulations may be made are set out in the FA 1986, s 104(1) and are where:

(a)   a potentially exempt transfer proves to be a chargeable transfer and, immediately before the death of the transferor, his estate includes property acquired by him from the transferee otherwise than for full consideration in money or money's worth;

(b)   an individual disposes of property by a transfer of value which is or proves to be a chargeable transfer as being property subject to a reservation to which the deceased was deemed to be beneficially entitled before his death or if the property has ceased to be subject to a reservation before his death it has become a potentially exempt transfer;

(c)   the 'artificial' debt provisions apply under s 103, or

(d)   the circumstances are such as may be specified in the regulations for the purposes of the subsection, being circumstances appearing to the Board to be similar to those referred to in (a)–(c) above.

2.74   The regulations may provide for treating the value transferred as being reduced by another transfer of value and/or giving a tax credit.

CHAPTER 3

Lifetime chargeable transfers and close companies

3.01 A lifetime transfer of value will not be potentially exempt unless it is made by an individual to another individual or is a gift by an individual into an accumulation and maintenance trust or a disabled trust (see para **2.04**). All other transfers of value chargeable in a person's lifetime, which for the purpose of this Guide are called 'lifetime chargeable transfers', will not qualify as potentially exempt transfers and the lifetime charge has been retained in respect of such transfers.

3.02 The objective of this chapter is to consider the provisions of the 1984 Act in so far as they apply specifically to lifetime chargeable transfers and the extent those provisions have been amended by the FA 1986. This will also involve considering the interaction of lifetime chargeable transfers with potentially exempt transfers. Finally, as gifts into and out of companies are treated as lifetime chargeable transfers, the application of inheritance tax to close companies will be very briefly considered.

The single tax Table

3.03 While before 18 March 1986 two tax Tables were prescribed, one for lifetime transfers and the other for transfers made within three years of death or on death, only one Table is now prescribed. The current Table commencing on 18 March 1986 is set out in Appendix B. The tax on the charge to lifetime chargeable transfers is now simply at half the death rates shown in the prescribed Table (substituted s 7(2) of the 1984 Act). Although the lifetime rates can be calculated by simply halving those applying in the prescribed Table, for convenience, particularly for the purpose of grossing-up, the same Appendix shows the tax payable at half the full rate.

Where transferor survives seven years

3.04 Tax is paid on lifetime chargeable transfers at the time they are made (unless falling within the nil band) on the value of the transfer at the date of the transfer and in accordance with the tax Table applying at the date of the transfer. If the transferor survives the transfer by seven years, then, unless he has reserved a benefit, no further tax becomes payable but neither, of course, is any tax refundable.

The tapered relief if death within seven years

3.05 If the transferor does not survive the gift by seven years, then the tax will have to be recalculated by applying the tax Table operating at the date of the transfer and not at the date of death. The tax payable will be at the full rate if the transferor has died within three years of making the transfer except, of course, credit will be given for any tax paid at the time of the making of the transfer. If the transferor has survived the gift by more than three years then the amount of tax payable is reduced by 20% on each of the successive years as in the case of potentially exempt transfers (see para **2.15**).

3.06 Additional tax therefore becomes payable on the difference between the revised amount of tax payable under this tapered relief and the tax originally paid. If the transferor has not survived the transfer by five years, the recalculated tax will be more than half the tabled rate. If the transferor has survived the gift by more than five years, the tax will normally be less, in which case this is ignored and there is no tax repayable.

3.07 However, even after the fifth year, additional tax may be payable if a reassessment of the transfer becomes necessary because there has been an earlier potentially exempt transfer made within seven years of the death (see para **2.20**) or if there has been a loss of business property relief or agricultural property relief if the transferee has disposed of the asset on which the relief was given within seven years of the transferor's death (see paras **7.12** and **7.59** respectively). In these cases the whole value of the gift will have to be recalculated, which will also affect any subsequent transfers and the estate.

Payment of the tax

3.08 Any additional tax which becomes payable resulting from the death of the transferor within seven years of the transfer is the primary liability of the transferee (see para **10.07**). The tax falls due six months after the end of the month in which the transferor's death occurs (see para **9.25**).

Relief for additional tax arising on lifetime chargeable transfers (s 131)

3.09 Where following the death of the transferor within seven years of the transfer, any additional tax which becomes payable in respect of the value transferred by a lifetime chargeable transfer is generally calculated by reference to the value actually transferred. However, relief is given by s 131 if the property transferred has been continously held by the transferee or his spouse when there has been a qualifying sale. The detailed conditions required to qualify for this relief are set out at para **4.06**.

Principal changes effected by the FA 1986

3.10 It may be helpful at this stage to summarise the principal changes contained in the FA 1986 which affect lifetime chargeable transfers:

(1) *The amount of tax payable.* This will initially still be half the full rate, but as outlined above more tax may become payable if the donor dies within seven years.

(2) *The cumulation period.* This has been reduced from ten to seven years (Sch 19, para 2(1)).

(3) *The gift with reservation provisions.* These apply to lifetime chargeable transfers as well as potentially exempt transfers as has already been outlined in Chapter 2.

(4) *Loss of business property and agricultural property relief.* These provisions requiring a lifetime transferee to have retained ownership of the transferred property within seven years before the transferor's death also extend to lifetime chargeable transfers (see paras **7.12** and **7.59**).

Differences between lifetime chargeable transfers and potentially exempt transfers

3.11 As a corollary of the principal changes effected by the FA 1986, it may be useful to consider the differences between the two types of transfer:

(1) Unless the lifetime chargeable transfer is within the nil band, the tax will be paid at the time of the transfer at half the full rate based on the tax Table applying at that time. This is subject to reassessment if the transferor dies within seven years. In the case of potentially exempt transfers, they are not taxed at all unless the transferor dies within seven years of the transfer, in which case while the value of the transfer is taken at the time it was made, the tax Table applied is that operating at the date of death.

(2) If the transferor survives a potentially exempt transfer by seven years, no tax is payable. In the case of a lifetime chargeable transfer, if tax has been paid on the transfer, it is not recoverable even if the transferor survives seven years.

(3) Both types of transfer are cumulated within the seven year period and are deemed to be made in the order in which they are actually made except for the limited purpose of applying the annual relief which is attracted first by the lifetime chargeable transfer in any one tax year (see para **2.13**).

(4) The grossing-up provisions considered in para **3.13** below do not apply in the case of potentially exempt transfers as no tax is paid on these transfers, if at all, until the transferor's death within seven years, in which case it is then normally borne by the transferee.

Reassessment of transfers

3.12 If the lifetime chargeable transfer is the first transfer made within seven years of the date of death of the transferor, it will normally not have to be re-assessed (except where the business property relief or agricultural property relief is lost, as outlined in para **3.10**(4) above), apart from applying the tapered relief. However, if the first lifetime transfer made within seven years of the death of the transferor is a potentially exempt transfer, then this is deemed to have been made at the time when it was made, which will therefore affect any subsequent lifetime chargeable transfers and potentially exempt transfers (see para **2.20**).

Grossing-up lifetime chargeable transfers

3.13 The logical consequence of the principle that the value transferred is the loss to the transferor's estate is the so-called 'grossing-up' rule. If the transferor agrees to pay the tax on the transfer, then the loss to his estate is the amount of the gift plus the tax on that tax, etc. This now only applies to lifetime chargeable transfers as opposed to potentially exempt transfers (except in the limited situation where the personal representatives actually have to pay the tax (see para **10.08**)) as the primary liability for the tax payable in the event of the transferor dying within the seven years falls on the transferee. The grossing-up rule may also be relevant when considering the application of exemptions on the distribution of an estate where specific tax free gifts have to be grossed up in certain situations (see para **10.33**).

The grossing-up calculation

3.14 The calculation is relatively simple where only one tax band is involved and where the net gift and the grossed-up value fall within the same band.

EXAMPLE

In September 1986, a settlor who has made no previous chargeable transfers but has utilised his annual exemptions, settles £75,000 into a discretionary trust and agrees to pay the tax. The amount taxable is therefore £4,000 on which tax is payable at 15%. The grossed-up amount on which the tax would be payable is therefore:

$$£4,000 \times \frac{100}{85} = 4,706,$$ on which tax of £706 is paid by the settlor

The gross value of the gift is therefore £75,706 which will now be the settlor's gross cumulative total.

This figure can also be calculated by referring to the half rates Table contained in Appendix B. The tax payable on the net gift shown in the 'Cumulative chargeable transfers (net)' column is the fraction shown in the 'Rate on net fraction' column. By referring to the Table, the grossed-up tax on the £4,000 (ie the first £4,000 in the band £71,000 – £91,400) is simply multiplied by the net fraction, ie £4,000 $\times$ $\frac{3}{17}$ths, which is £706. This therefore makes the total cumulative gross transfers to date £75,706 (ie the net gift of £75,000 + £706).

Where transfer spans more than one tax band

3.15 Where the grossing-up extends the gross value of the transfer into a higher band than the net transfer, the calculation becomes more complex and the most convenient method of calculating the tax is by using the grossing-up Table as outlined above.

EXAMPLE

The same settlor in the last example, a month later transfers a further £20,000 to a close company. He has already made gross transfers totalling £75,706.

If the transferee pays the tax, then this will simply be calculated on the rates appropriate between £75,706 and £95,706, viz £19,294 at 15% and £706 at $17\frac{1}{2}$% = £2,894 + 124 = £3,018.

If, however, the transferor agrees to pay the tax, then it must be grossed-up. To use the 'Cumulative chargeable transfers (net)' column, it is essential therefore to consider the transferor's cumulative net transfers to date and not the gross transfers. The transferor has made net transfers of £75,000 when he now makes a further net transfer of £20,000. Of this further net transfer, £16,400 falls within the first chargeable band (£91,400–£75,000) and the balance of £3,600 falls within the second chargeable band.

The tax is therefore calculated as $\frac{3}{17}$ths of £16,400 plus $\frac{7}{33}$rds of £3,600 = £2,894 + £764 = £3,658.

Tax of £3,658 is therefore paid by the transferor.

The transferor's gross cumulative total is therefore now £75,000 + £706 + £20,000 + £3,658 = £99,364.

CLOSE COMPANIES (ss 94–101)

3.16 Transfers of value to a company and dispositions by a company apportioned between the participants do not qualify as potentially exempt transfers and are therefore to be treated as lifetime chargeable transfers.

3.17 While a company can make a transfer of value, it cannot make a chargeable transfer of value, as this can only be made by an individual (s 2(1)).

3.18 In the absence of any special provisions, this would mean that a company could be used as a means of making tax free gifts. This could be a direct gift of the company's assets. Alternatively, for example, shares in a company of £1 nominal value, but actually worth £10 per share, could be issued by the company at par (provided there is no restrictions to prevent this in the Articles of Association) to the intended beneficiaries. As the disposition of the shares is by the company it would not attract a charge to tax.

Apportionment of transfers between participants (s 94(1))

3.19 Accordingly, s 94(1) apportions any transfer of value made by a close company between the participants according to their respective rights and interests in the company immediately before the transfer.

3.20 It will be therefore necessary to first ascertain whether the company has made a transfer of value resulting in a loss to the company under s 3(1), as already considered in Chapter 1. While such a transfer of value cannot be a chargeable transfer of value, nevertheless, the loss suffered by the company will be apportioned between the participants. The same would apply if the company deliberately omits to exercise a right, such as failing to enforce payment of a debt.

The effect

3.21 Accordingly, under s 94(1), each individual to whom the company's transfer of value is apportioned is treated as if that individual has made a transfer of value of the net amount; this will therefore involve a grossing-up unless the transferee pays the tax. The usual exemptions apply, such as if the transfer is to the participant's spouse or to a charity. The apportioned grossed-up sum then has to be cumulated with any earlier chargeable transfers of the individual for ascertaining the inheritance tax on subsequent chargeable transfers. An exception is made for a person to whom not more than 5% of the value transferred by the company is apportioned. While the net amount apportioned is grossed-up at its marginal rate of tax in the normal way to ascertain the tax payable on the disposition by the company, the grossed-up amount is not cumulated with any subsequent chargeable transfers (s 94(4)).

Alterations in capital (s 98)

3.22 Where there is an alteration in a close company's unquoted share or loan capital or an alteration in any rights attaching to unquoted shares in or debentures of a close company, the alterations are deemed to have been disposals by the participants and apportioned among them.

Interests in settled property (ss 99–101)

3.23 Where a close company is entitled to an interest in possession in settled property, the persons who are participants in relation to the company are treated for the purposes of inheritance tax as being persons beneficially entitled to the interest in possession according to their respective rights and interests in the company (s 101). Where the shares are held by the trustees of a settlement without an interest in possession, provisions for charging are incorporated in ss 99–100.

3.24 Accordingly, these provisions broadly equate transfers of value made by the company as being chargeable transfers of value by the participants pro rata to their entitlement in the company.

3.25 It is beyond the scope of this Guide to deal with the close company provisions in detail, but now that transfers of value to and dispositions by companies do not qualify as potentially exempt transfers, there is a further disincentive to use companies as a means of transferring capital.

CHAPTER 4

Inheritance tax on death

Introduction

4.01 The objective of this chapter is to collate into one chapter the principles of the charge to inheritance tax where they apply on a death and also to consider the exemptions and special valuation provisions which are only applicable to a transfer on death.

4.02 On the death of a person domiciled in the UK, tax is charged as if, immediately before his death, he had made a transfer of value equal to the value of his estate immediately before his death. No grossing up is necessary, the tax being paid out of the estate before distribution.

4.03 With the exception of gifts subject to a reservation, any lifetime transfers are not treated as having taken place on death, but the subsequent death of the transferor may still affect lifetime transfers, which will also be relevant to the marginal rate of tax on the estate itself.

THE RELEVANCE OF LIFETIME TRANSFERS

4.04 On death, therefore, the following matters will have to be considered by the earlier transferees and the personal representatives to enable them to assess their respective tax liabilities resulting from the death:

(1) *Potentially exempt transfers.* If death occurs within seven years of such a transfer, or a reservation of benefit to the donor ceases during that period converting it into a potentially exempt transfer, then such transfers become chargeable transfers (see para **2.07**). As such they are deemed to have been effected on the date on which the transfer was made, but the rate of tax applying to those transfers will be the rate applicable at the date of death with a tapered relief after the third year (see para **2.12**). This may require a reassessment of subsequent lifetime transfers as illustrated in para **2.20**.

(2) *Lifetime chargeable transfers.* If death occurs within seven years of such transfers, then again they are deemed to have taken place on the day on which they actually occurred and the tax on those transfers may have to be reassessed. The tax will be based on the rate applying at the date of the transfer, but reduced in accordance with a tapered relief after the third year (see para **3.05**). If tax has been paid on the transfer, this will have been paid at the lower lifetime rate; if this has been at half the death rate, normally no more tax would then become payable if the transferor has survived five years. However, even if more than five years have elapsed since the date of the transfer, further tax may still arise if there has been an earlier potentially exempt transfer within the seven years from the date of death which requires reassessment of subsequent transfers (see para **2.20**) or if business property relief or agricultural property relief is lost as outlined immediately below.

(3) *Loss of business or agricultural property relief.* If the transferee makes a lifetime disposition of property attracting business property relief or agricultural property relief within seven years of the transferor's death, the relief will be lost which will necessitate a reassessment of that transfer and all subsequent transfers (see paras **7.12** and **7.59** respectively).

(4) *Political parties.* Transfers to political parties are wholly exempt if the donor survives a gift by the year, but otherwise they are only exempt to the extent of £100,000 (see para **5.13**). The burden of this additional tax falls on the transferee, but it may also necessitate a reassessment of any subsequent lifetime transfers and, of course, in any event will increase the marginal rate of tax on the estate.

(6) *Cumulation.* Both types of lifetime transfer are cumulated in the seven year period before the date of death. This will clearly affect the point on the scale at which the estate is taxed, as effectively the estate will bear the full brunt of the marginal rate of tax with any other assets which are aggregated with the free estate (see para **9.02**).

(6) *Gifts with reservation.* Such gifts are treated as property to which the donor is beneficially entitled immediately before the date of his death and as such are aggregated with his estate (see para **2.28**). These are also considered below in para **4.10**.

(7) *Inheritance (Provision for Family and Dependents) Act 1975.* Where a transfer of value is undone by an order made under this Act, any tax is repaid or, if unpaid, ceases to be payable. The transfer on death is charged as if the previous transfer had not been made but, of course, any money

recovered for the estate does form part of the estate for the purpose of the transfer on death (s 146).

(8) *Transfers reported late.* Where a transfer of value has not been notified to the Inland Revenue, or only discovered by them after payment has been accepted in full satisfaction of the tax due on the later transfer, the tax due on the earlier transfer is charged as if it had been effected after the later transfer (see para **9.03** for reportable lifetime transfers). Where, however, the later transfer is made on death then the earlier transfer is treated as having been made immediately before the death. The effect of these provisions, now contained in s 264, is that the earlier later-reported transfer will therefore lose the advantage of utilising the nil rate or lower bands of tax, which will already have been utilised by the subsequent transfers. Furthermore, where the late reporting or discovery does not occur until after the death of the transferor, then the death rates are now applied irrespective of when the transfer was actually made. The moral is to ensure that transfers are not reported late! Potentially exempt transfers do not have to be reported in the transferor's lifetime, as they do not become chargeable unless and until the transferor fails to survive the transfer by seven years.

The burden of tax

4.05 Any tax, or additional tax, that becomes payable in respect of lifetime transfers is borne by the respective transferees not by the estate (see paras **10.07** and **10.09**). This is a factor which a testator will have to keep in mind when drafting his will under which he may wish to direct that the additional tax should be borne out of his estate. Such a direction will be equivalent to a legacy of the amount of tax payable.

Relief for additional tax arising on lifetime transfers (s 131)

4.06 Where, following the death of the transferor within seven years of the transfer, any tax becomes chargeable in respect of the value transferred by a potentially exempt transfer, or any additional tax becomes payable in respect of the value transferred by any other chargeable transfer, tax is generally calculated by reference to the value actually transferred. However, relief is given by virtue of s 131 in two circumstances: if the property transferred has since the transfer either:

(a) been held continuously by the transferee or his spouse up to the date of death of the transferor, when the value at the date of death may be substituted if less; or

(b)   been sold by the transferee or his spouse by a qualifying sale before the date of death of the transferor, when the sale price may be substituted.

If the value of the property was reduced by business property or agricultural property relief at the time of the transfer, the value at death is reduced by the same percentage (s 131(2A) inserted by the FA 1986, Sch 19, para 23(3)). This is subject, of course, to the reliefs not being lost by virtue of the transferee making a lifetime disposal of the relieved property within seven years of the transferor's death (see paras **7.12** and **7.59**).

Qualifying sale

4.07   A qualifying sale for the purpose of (b) above is one if:

(a)   it is at arm's length for a price freely negotiated at the time of the sale; and
(b)   no person concerned as vendor (or as having an interest in the proceeds of the sale) is the same as or connected with any person concerned as purchaser (or as having an interest in the purchase); and
(c)   no provision is made in, or in connection with, the agreement for the sale, that the vendor (or any person having an interest in the proceeds of sale) is to have any right to acquire some or all of the property sold or some interest in or created out of it.

Relief limited to tax arising on the death

4.08   Where the lower figure is substituted for the value at the date of the transfer under this relief, for the purposes of a potentially exempt transfer, the value is reduced in respect of the whole tax payable. In the case of a lifetime chargeable transfer, the lower figure is substituted for the purpose only of the additional tax which becomes payable on a death, not in respect of the original tax that was paid (s 131(1) as amended by the FA 1986, Sch 19, para 23).

Wasting and replacement assets

4.09   The relief under s 131 does not apply if the transferred property was tangible moveable property that is a wasting asset (s 132). Special rules cover situations in which the property changes between the date of transfer and the death of the transferor or the qualifying sale as the case may be; this may arise, for example, if there has been a script issue or a re-organisation of share capital, etc. If the interest is an interest in land and is not at both critical dates the same in all respects, the market value is increased or reduced to take account of what its value would have been if it had remained unaltered (s 137). In the case of a lease not exceeding 50 years, a formula to adjust the value is contained in s 138. With regard to other property which is not in all respects the same as at the time of the transfer and the relevant date, the market value is ascertained as if the change had not occurred: these provisions are set out in s 139.

The estate and assets aggregated with the estate

4.10 Where a person dies, tax is charged as if immediately before his death, he had made a transfer of value equal to the value of his estate immediately before his death. While this will include the free estate and property passing by survivorship, the inheritance tax net is somewhat wider. The total of all the following must be aggregated together for the purpose of ascertaining the tax payable and then the tax rateably apportioned between the interests:

(1) *The deceased's free estate.* Assets owned beneficially by the deceased clearly form part of his estate;

(2) *Property passing by survivorship.* Tax is imposed on the estate in existence immediately before the deceased's death, which therefore includes property passing by survivorship on the death. This would apply to a beneficial joint tenancy of any property, whether land, bank accounts, etc, if the benefit of the deceased's beneficial share passes by survivorship;

(3) *Interests in possession in settlements.* It is provided by s 49(1) that a person beneficially entitled to an interest in possession in settled property shall be treated as beneficially entitled to the property in which the interest subsists. Further s 51(1) provides that where such a person disposes of his interest, tax is charged as if at that time he had made a transfer of value equal to the value of the property in which his interest subsists. The value of the trust funds in which the interest subsists will therefore be aggregated with the estate for this purpose. The expression 'interest in possession' is not defined in the Act, but broadly is an interest where a person has the present right to enjoy the present income from the property or possession of it, the simplest illustration being a life interest. It will therefore not include the beneficiary of a discretionary settlement.

(4) *General power of appointment.* Assets over which the deceased had a *general* power of appointment are treated as his own for this purpose.

(5) *Property subject to reservation.* Gifted property which is still subject to a reservation in favour of the donor at the date of death.

Illustration

4.11   This can be illustrated with an example.

EXAMPLE
D, who has made no previous transfers, makes a gift of £77,000 to his
son in 1984. In 1985 he gives his daughter his property valued at
£100,000, but which he continues to occupy rent free up to the date of
his death. D and his brother also own Blackacre as beneficial joint
tenants and which, at the date of D's death in August 1986, is valued
at £60,000. D also has a power of appointment over funds worth
£10,000. On D's death he has a life interest in settled funds valued at
£40,000 and leaves a free estate of £66,000. The total chargeable assets
are therefore:

	£
House	100,000
Half share in Blackacre	30,000
Appointed funds	10,000
Settled funds	40,000
Free estate	66,000
Aggregated chargeable assets	246,000

As the lifetime gift to the son has exactly utilised the nil band
(allowing for £6,000 annual reliefs), the tax payable will be calculated
on total transfers of £317,000 (£71,000 plus £246,000), viz £110,500.
This tax will be apportioned pro rata to the chargeable aggregated
assets. So, for example, the tax on the house will be:

$$100,000 \times \frac{110,500}{246,000} = 44,919$$

If a large number of assets are involved, it may be more convenient
to ascertain the 'estate rate' which is then applied to each asset in turn
to calculate the tax attributable to that asset.

$$\frac{\text{Tax payable}}{\text{Total chargeable assets aggregated}} = \frac{110,500}{246,000} \times 100 = 44.919\% = \text{estate rate}$$

Each chargeable asset will therefore bear tax at the estate rate, so in
the same example, the estate rate applied to the value of the house is
simply £44,919.

Burden of tax

4.12　As illustrated above, tax on the assets aggregated with the free estate is borne by the respective beneficiaries or funds. This is a factor which a testator will have to keep in mind when drafting his will under which he may wish to direct that the tax on any particular assets or funds should be borne out of his free estate. This may be particularly relevant to property passing by survivorship. Such a direction will be equivalent to a legacy of the amount of the tax payable.

Exclusions from the estate including summary of exemptions

4.13　The following assets or interests are not included in the estate for inheritance tax purposes:

(1) *Assets acquired posthumously.*
(2) *Gifts saved from lapse.*　By virtue of the Wills Act 1837, s 33 (as amended by the Administration of Estates Act 1982) where there is a gift to a child or other issue of the testator who predeceases the testator leaving issue surviving the testator, the gift is saved from lapse and now passes direct to the issue (previously it passed to the deceased beneficiary's estate). It is therefore treated as a direct gift to the issue who take.
(3) *Commorientes.*　By virtue of LPA 1925, s 184, where persons die in circumstances rendering it uncertain who has survived the other, then those persons are deemed to die in order of seniority. A younger person will therefore be deemed to have outlived an older person who dies in similar circumstances. Strictly the older person's estate should pass to the younger person's and then on to the beneficiaries under the younger person's will or intestacy. However by virtue of s 4(2), the older person's estate is deemed to pass direct to the beneficiaries under the younger person's estate. This only applies where there is uncertainty as to the order of death; if the order of death is known, then it will pass through both estates accordingly. While quick succession relief may be available in these circumstances (see para **4.28**) this may still substantially increase the survivor's estate so attracting the higher bands of tax. To avoid this, a contingency clause should be inserted (see (14) below).
(4) *Property situate outside the UK.*　Property situate outside the UK, where the person beneficially entitled to it is an individual domiciled outside the UK, is excluded property and does not form part of the estate (see para **1.18**).
(5) *Reversionary interests.*　Such interests which have not yet fallen into possession are by virtue of s 48 excluded property

except in certain circumstances (see para **1.22**). This differs from previous estate duty provisions whereby such interests were treated as part of the estate and an election could be made whether to pay the tax on the death or when the reversionary interest fell into possession (see para **0.02**).

(6) *Reverter to settlor.* Where a person is entitled to an interest in possession in settled property which on his death, but during the settlor's lifetime, reverts to the settlor, the value of the settled property is left out of account in determining the value of the deceased's estate (s 54(1)). For the purpose of this and the immediately following head, where it cannot be known which of two or more persons who have died survived the other or others, they shall be assumed to have died at the same instant. So if, for example, the person entitled to the interest in possession is younger than the settlor, the normal commorientes rule under s 184 referred to under (3) above does not apply so that this relief is not lost.

(7) *Reverter to settlor's spouse.* Where on the death of a person entitled to an interest in possession in settled property the settlor's spouse or, if the settlor has died less than two years earlier, the settlor's widow or widower, becomes entitled to the settled property and is domiciled in the UK, the value of the settled property is left out of account (s 54(2)).

(8) *Superannuation funds.* A right to a pension or annuity under approved funds shall be left out of account in determining the value of a person's estate provided it does not result from the application of any benefit provided otherwise than by way of a pension or annuity (eg a lump sum). The conditions are laid down under s 151.

(9) *Conditional exemption.* Works of art and other objects and land may enjoy conditional exemption on transfer on death. If they qualify they are left out of account (see para **5.31**). This relief must be claimed.

(10) *Timber.* The value of timber may be left out of account until such time as the timber is sold but an election must be made in this case (see para **7.75**).

(11) *Surviving spouse exemption.* Where under the estate duty provisions property was settled on a spouse for life with gifts over, tax was paid on the first death, but not on the death of the surviving spouse. Where this exemption has been earned in respect of deaths before 13 November 1974, it will continue to apply under inheritance tax (see para **0.02(3)**).

(12) *Exempt transfers.* As in the case of lifetime gifts, a number of transfers are exempt. These are described in Chapter 5 and

include in particular gifts between spouses and to charities. Other types of lifetime transfers, such as the annual, small gifts, marriage gifts and the normal and reasonable expenditure exemptions do not apply on death.

(13) *Dispositions which are not transfers of value.* On death there is a deemed transfer of value, but not a deemed disposition, so these exemptions (see para **1.34**) do not apply on a death, except, perhaps, waiver of remuneration or of dividends can be incorporated in the will without causing the waived interest to become chargeable.

(14) *Survivorship clauses.* If a will provides for a survivorship clause not exceeding six months, then the legacy does not form part of the contingent beneficiary's estate (s 92).

Death on active service (s 154)

4.14 Apart from the exemptions summarised above, there is a further exemption which only applies on a death. This is where a person is certified by the Ministry of Defence to have died:

(a) from a wound inflicted, accident occurring or disease contracted at a time when he or she was a member of the armed forces on active service against an enemy or other service of a warlike nature; or

(b) from a disease contracted at some previous time, the death being due or hastened by the aggravation of the disease during the period which he or she was in such active service.

Service in Northern Ireland qualifies and by concession the relief has been extended to estates of members of the Royal Ulster Constabulary who die from injuries caused by terrorist activity in Northern Ireland. This exemption also extends to the estates of persons killed on active service in the Falkland Islands.

It will therefore be appreciated that the relief is not limited to where persons are killed on active service or even still a member of the armed forces; the only requirement is that the wound was inflicted, or the accident occurred, or the disease contracted, while on active service, or that the previously contracted disease was aggravated while on active service.

The case of the Fourth Duke of Westminster

4.15 The extent of this relief had to be considered in the case of the death of the Fourth Duke of Westminster: *Barty-King v Ministry of Defence*. The claim for exemption in that case was under the FA 1972, s 71, which contains virtually an identical provision to s 154. The issue of contention in that case was the casual connection between a wound suffered by the Duke in the Second World War in 1944, when he was wounded in France while in action against the enemy, and his death in 1967. The Duke left an estate of several million pounds and his executors applied for a certificate from the Ministry of Defence under the FA 1952, s 71. After failing a number of times to obtain a certificate, the executors then applied to the High Court for a declaration that a certificate should be issued.

The executors contended that the wound caused a cancer from which the Duke had died, but the cancer had been masked by other complications; if the cancer had been diagnosed and had received timely treatment, the Duke's chances of survival would have been four to one in his favour. Further, the wound seriously affected his left leg causing septicaemia and lowering his resistance to infection. The Ministry of Defence contended that the exemption did not apply where death, not directly caused by the wound, takes place sooner than it might have done if the wound had not been suffered.

May J held that, for the purposes of this exemption, it was not necessary for the wound directly, pathologically or psychologically to have brought about the death. Questions of causation were often extremely difficult, but a commonsense approach had to be taken. The wound did not have to be the only cause of death. The Ministry of Defence found that the Duke had suffered from septicaemia which, although not a direct pathological cause, significantly contributed to the death. In the circumstances, the Duke's executors were entilted to a certificate even though he had survived for twenty-three years after the wound had been inflicted.

Review of earlier cases

4.16 Following this decision, the Secretary of State for Defence has issued a statement that a review has been authorised of previously unsuccessful applications. In each case where the papers are still held, it will be reconsidered. The papers have not been retained in cases where the applications were made more than ten years ago, but these cases will be reconsidered if a fresh application is made with supporting evidence.

Exemption extends to all charges on death

4.17 This exemption extends to all situations where there may be a charge to tax on death, such as where the deceased was a beneficial joint tenant or had a life interest in a settled fund. In view of the fact that total exemption is given in this situation, if under a will or on intestacy the estate passes to an exempt transferee, one should carefully consider varying the will to ensure that it passes to transferees who can benefit from the exemption.

VALUATION OF THE ESTATE ON DEATH

Valuation made after death

4.18   While the deceased is deemed to have made a transfer of value equal to the value of his estate immediately before his death, with regard to the valuation of the assets, the general rule is that the valuation is made after the death (s 171). This means that changes in the value of the estate which have occurred by reason of the death are taken into account as if they had occurred before the death.

Changes resulting from death

4.19   Such changes would therefore ensure that additions to the property comprised in the estate, such as lump sums payable under pension schemes and damages recoverable under the Law Reform Miscellaneous Provisions Act 1934 for loss of expectation of life would be included. Further, any increase or decrease in the value of the estate resulting from the death will be taken into account, such as the value of a life policy (which only has a surrender value immediately before death), in contrast to an annuity which ceases on death. Further, the death of a proprietor or a partner of a business may cause loss of goodwill which is a consideration in valuing the business or partnership. An exception to this valuation rule is that on the death of a joint tenant whose interest passes to the survivors, the fact of death is ignored as otherwise the value would be nil (s 171(2)).

Valuation of debts due to the estate (s 166)

4.20   Any moneys due to the estate will form part of the estate. In determining the value of a right to receive a sum due under any obligation, it is assumed that the obligation wil be duly discharged, except if and to the extent that recovery of the sum is impossible or not reasonably practical and has not become so by any act or omission of the person to whom the sum is due. This means, for example, that if a debt is due to the estate at the date of death and could reasonably have been recovered at that time, it will form part of the value of the estate notwithstanding that subsequently it may become statute-barred.

Liabilities of the estate

4.21 On death a person is deemed to have made a transfer of value of the whole of his estate and therefore when valuing the estate, the liabilities are generally to be taken into account unless they have been created voluntarily or artificially to reduce the value of the estate.

Funeral expenses and foreign property

4.22 Although incurred after the death, reasonable funeral expenses may be deducted from the value of the estate (s 172) as may expenses (not exceeding 5%) incurred in connection with administering or realising property situate outside the UK (s 173).

Outstanding inheritance tax liability

4.23 Any outstanding inheritance tax liability incurred before the date of death is allowed to the extent only that it is actually paid out (s 174(2)).

Liabilities incurred during administration

4.24 Debts or liabilities incurred by the personal representatives, such as the administration expenses, or incurred by the beneficiaries, such as the cost of a gravestone, are not liabilities of the deceased and therefore are not deductible in calculating the value of the estate before death.

4.25 Otherwise, a debt of the estate is normally deductible from its value provided (except in the case of a liability imposed by law) it was incurred for a consideration in money or money's worth and provided it has not been created artificially.

Summary of liabilities which are disallowed

4.26 The extent to which liabilities are allowed to reduce the value of the transfer are considered in Chapter 6 (paras **6.33** to **6.48**), but it may be helpful at this stage to summarise these provisions so far as they apply on a death:

(a)   under s 5(5), a debt is not deductible unless it is a liability imposed by law or was incurred for a consideration of money or money's worth (see para **6.34**);

(b)   a debt is not deductible to the extent that neither the executor nor anyone else is liable to pay the debt nor is it charged on any property as in *Re Barnes* (see para **6.45**);

(c)   'artificial' debts are effectively partially or wholly disallowed by virtue of the FA 1986, s 103, (see paras **6.37** to **6.43**).

Reliefs available on death

4.27 The general reliefs applying to lifetime transfers extend to transfers on death. These are dealt with in Chapter 7 and are:

(i) business property relief (see para **7.02**); and
(ii) agricultural property relief (see para **7.26**).

4.28 There are two further reliefs which are only available on death. The first of these is woodlands relief, also dealt with in Chapter 7 (see para **7.75**). The second is quick succession relief.

Quick succession relief

4.29 This relief is given where a person dies within five years of receiving a chargeable transfer whether by lifetime gift or on death, on which tax has been paid. The relief given is by way of a tax credit in the deceased's estate which is calculated by ascertaining the tax attributable to the increase in the recipient's estate. The amount of credit given is the tax so ascertained which is given in full if the death occurs within one year of the transfer and thereafter the relief is reduced by 20% on each of the successive years as follows:

Period between transfer and death	*Percentage available*
One year or less	100
Between 1 and 2 years	80
Between 2 and 3 years	60
Between 3 and 4 years	40
Between 4 and 5 years	20
More than 5 years	Nil

The relief available may be calculated as follows:

$$\frac{\text{Net gift}}{\text{Gross gift}} \times \text{tax paid on original transfer} \times \text{percentage available} = \text{tax credit}$$

EXAMPLE
A father, who has made no previous transfers, dies in April 1986 leaving his estate of £95,000 to his son on which tax of £7,200 is paid leaving £87,800 net for the son. The son is killed in May 1987 having made no previous lifetime transfers and leaving an estate of £164,000 which he gives to his children. Without allowing for any indexation in the tax table of May 1987, tax on the son's estate will be £33,100 less the quick succession relief which is arrived at as follows:

$$\frac{87,800}{95,000} \times 7,200 \times \frac{80}{100} = £5,323$$

So the tax payable on the son's estate will be £33,100 – £5,323 = £27,777.

Tax credit

4.30   This relief is therefore a credit of tax charged on the first transfer against the tax due on the second transfer and which is attributable to the increase in the present estate. As it is a credit on tax paid on the first transfer, if no tax was paid on the earlier transfer then, of course, no credit will be due. Conversely, if the tax credit exceeds the amount of tax due on the present estate, then there will be no repayment of the balance which will therefore be wasted. Furthermore, as it is a tax credit, it does not operate to reduce the value of the estate, but is merely a credit given against any tax payable.

SPECIAL VALUATION RELIEFS ON DEATH

4.31   Normally the value of assets included in an estate is taken to be the value at the date of death. To this there are three principal exceptions.

Sale of qualifying shares within 12 months (ss 178–189)

4.32   Where qualifying investments are sold within 12 months of death for less than their probate value, then the gross proceeds of sale may be substituted for the probate value. If a claim for relief is made under these provisions, the value of all shares sold within the 12 months must be taken into account and not merely those which have resulted in a loss.

Qualifying investment

4.33   A qualifying investment is defined by s 178(1) as, broadly, shares or securities which are quoted on a recognised stock exchange, holdings in an authorised unit trust and shares in any common investment fund. The costs of sale are disregarded so that it is only the gross proceeds which may be substituted for the probate value.

Sale by the 'appropriate person'

4.34   The sale must be by the appropriate person, which is the person who is liable for the tax on the relevant investments. This will normally be the personal representatives or the trustees of a settlement in which the deceased had an interest in possession at the date of his death. This means that care must be taken to ensure that investments standing at a loss are sold by the correct person. The relief therefore would not be available, for example, where the personal representatives vested the shares in the beneficiaries who are not liable to pay the tax and it is they who then subsequently make the loss.

Sales and repurchases within 12 months of death

4.35 There are further provisions to cover the situation where qualifying investments have been sold within 12 months of the death, but a repurchase is made within two months of the last qualifying sale. In that event the loss is proportionately reduced as follows:

$$\frac{\text{Gross cost of reinvestments}}{\begin{array}{l}\text{Gross proceeds of sale of}\\ \text{original investments}\end{array}} \times \text{loss} = \text{amount of relief lost}$$

EXAMPLE
Comprised in an estate are qualifying investments at a probate value of £100,000. These are all sold by the executors six months later at £60,000 and a month later £30,000 is reinvested in qualifying investments. But for the repurchase, the relief would have been £40,000, but in view of the repurchase it must be reduced as follows:

$$\frac{£30,000}{£60,000} \times 40,000 = 20,000$$

The loss will therefore be limited to £40,000 − £20,000 = £20,000.

4.36 This curtailment of the loss can be avoided by waiting two months after the last qualifying sale before making any reinvestment. Alternatively, as it is only sales within the period of 12 months from the date of death which are considered, if shares are sold at a loss immediately before the end of the 12 months, then reinvestment may be made immediately after the year has elapsed as the reinvestments are not then made within the 12 months.

Other provisions

4.37 Detailed provisions are incorporated in the remainder of Chapter III of Pt VI of the Act dealing with capital receipts, payment of calls, changes in holdings, exchanges, attribution of values to specific investments for capital gains tax purposes, etc.

Sale of land within three years of death (ss 190–198)

4.38 Where an interest in land is comprised in a person's estate and sold for less than the probate value within three years of the date of death, then the gross sale price may be substituted for the probate value, subject to a number of qualifications set out in Chapter IV of Pt VI of the Act.

Sale by 'qualifying person'

4.39 The sale must be by a qualifying person, that is the person who is liable to pay the tax. If it is sold by any other person, then the relief will not be available. If, therefore, the personal representatives are liable to pay the tax and they subsequently sell it at below probate value, then the sale price can be substituted for the probate value. On the other hand, if the personal representatives first assent the property into the name of the beneficiary and the beneficiary subsequently sells at a loss, then the relief is lost.

Land excludes mortgages, etc

4.40 Land is not defined, but it expressly excludes any estate interest or right by way of mortgage or other security (s 190(1)).

Minimum claim

4.41 There is a *de minimis* provision that if the sale value differs from the probate value by less than the lower of £1,000 or 5% of the probate value, no claim for relief is available.

Sale to beneficiary excluded

4.42 The relief is excluded if the sale by a personal representative or a trustee is to a person who has been beneficially entitled to an interest in the property since the date of death or who is the spouse or remoter issue of such a person. Likewise, the relief is excluded if the sale is by the trustees of a settlement to any such persons beneficially entitled to an interest in the land under the settlement.

4.43 This relief must be claimed.

Sales and repurchases within three years of death

4.44 If the qualifying person having made the sale then, within three years of the date of death, purchases another property or properties, within four months of the last of the sales, and if the cost of the new properties is the same or more than realised on the sales within the three years, then no claim is available. If, however, the total cost of such repurchases in the three years is less than the amount realised from the earlier sale, then by virtue of s 192 the relief is reduced by the appropriate fraction as follows:

$$\frac{\text{Purchase price of new properties}}{\text{Sale price of all property sold in the three years}} = \text{appropriate fraction}$$

EXAMPLE

A property valued at £150,000 for probate is sold within three years from the date of death at £120,000. Within four months of the sale, one third of the proceeds (£40,000) are reinvested. The relief on the loss of £30,000 is reduced by the appropriate fraction as follows:

$$\frac{40,000}{120,000} = \frac{1}{3}$$

So, the relief is reduced by one third of the £30,000 (i.e. £10,000) resulting in the relief being reduced to £20,000.

4.45   This loss of reduction in the relief can be avoided by ensuring that any repurchases are not made until four months have elapsed since the date of the last sale or, alternatively, as the relief is only lost in respect of repurchases within the three-year period, if the sales are made shortly before the three years from date of death, the repurchases can be made immediately after the three years from the date of death.

4.46   Further, this reduction only applies where a purchase is made by the person liable to pay the tax. It would therefore not apply where, for example, a beneficiary had made a subsequent purchase.

4.47   If the nature of an interest in land alters between the date of death and the date of the qualifying sale, adjustments for this have to be made in accordance with s 193 by endeavouring to ascertain what the value of the property would have been if the circumstances prevailing at the date of the sale had prevailed immediately before the death.

Other provisions

4.48   The remaining sections in Chapter IV of Pt VI of the Act deal with the position of changes between death and sale, wasting leases of 50 years or less where appropriate adjustment has to be made and anti-avoidance provisions with regard to sales to beneficiaries and exchanges.

Sale of related property within three years of death (s 176)

4.49   Where the value of property comprised in an estate has been increased by virtue of the related property provisions under s 161, if there is a sale of the property within three years of death, in certain circumstances, if the sale price is lower, the asset may be valued in isolation from the related property rules. This is considered in further detail in para **6.23**.

CHAPTER 5

Exemptions

Introduction

5.01 This chapter considers the 'true' exemptions from inheritance tax, that is dispositions which are transfers of value and would otherwise be chargeable transfers but for the statutory exemption given.

5.02 Exemption may also effectively be given by declaring the asset or interest involved to be excluded property and therefore not forming part of the transferor's estate. These are property situate outside the UK being owned by a person not domiciled in the UK (see para **1.18**) and reversionary interests (see para **1.22**).

5.03 Exemption may also be achieved by declaring certain dispositions not to be transfers of value (see para **1.34**).

5.04 Inheritance tax is payable on a chargeable transfer, which is any transfer of value made by an individual, other than an exempt transfer (s 2).

5.05 A transfer may be wholly exempt, such as transfers between spouses, or only limited to a specific amount, such as the annual exemption £3,000.

5.06 A transfer of value may attract exemption on the basis that it is a disposition to an exempt transferee, or alternatively, it may attract exemption because it falls within a category of limited lifetime transfers.

EXEMPT TRANSFEREES

Transfers between spouses (s 18)

5.07 Transfers of value between spouses are wholly exempt where:

(a)   both parties are domiciled in the UK; or

(b)   if both parties are domiciled outside the UK; or

(c)   if the transferee only is domiciled in the UK.

If the transferor is domiciled in the UK and the transferee spouse outside the UK, then the spouse exemption only applies up to the first £55,000 (this figure no longer follows the nil rate band).

These restrictions apply to prevent a UK domiciled spouse giving assets to his foreign domiciled spouse tax free, who then makes the intended gift while domiciled outside the UK.

Extends to absolute and settled gifts

5.08 This exemption extends to transfers where an interest in possession passes between the spouses. The exemption therefore applies regardless of whether the gift is outright or settled.

Meaning of spouse

5.09 A spouse is not defined in the 1984 Act. The restrictions that apply for income tax and capital gains tax purposes that spouses should be living together do not apply to inheritance tax. The test is therefore under the general law whether the parties are legally married. A void marriage cannot be regarded as a marriage for this purpose at any time, whereas parties continue to be spouses until such time as there is a decree of divorce absolute or in the case of a voidable marriage a decree of nullity. It would appear that the parties to a valid polygamous marriage, that is one recognised as valid by the personal law of the parties, are to be regarded as spouses for the purpose of this exemption. In *Re Sehota*, one of two surviving widows of a polygamous marriage was held to be a 'wife' within the meaning of s 1(1)(a) of the Inheritance (Provision for Family and Dependants) Act 1975. In principle there is no reason why this should not be extended to inheritance tax for the purpose of this exemption.

Conditions

5.10 There are two conditions imposed. The exemption is lost if *either*:

(a)   the disposition takes effect on the termination after the transfer of value of any interest or period. This condition therefore effectively requires the spouse to take an immediate interest in possession. So, for example, if a testator leaves property to his son for two years and then to his widow, this first condition is not satisfied. It is, however, expressly provided that relief is not lost by reason only that the property is given to a spouse contingently on surviving the deceased by not more than 12 months (this is therefore longer than the normal contingency period allowed of six months under s 92); *or*

(b) the disposition depends on a condition which is not satisfied within 12 months after the transfer.

Charities (s 23)

5.11 There is no longer any limit on the amount that can be given to charity during one's lifetime or on death and gifts to charities are therefore now wholly exempt up to any amount provided certain restrictions are not breached.

Conditions

5.12 To prevent abuse of this exemption, a number of conditions are imposed. The exemption will be lost if *any* of the following apply to the gift (the first two being the same as the transfers to a spouse):

(a) the disposition takes effect on the termination after the transfer of value of any interest or period; or

(b) the disposition depends on a condition which is not satisfied within 12 months after the transfer; or

(c) the disposition is defeasible. However, for this purpose, if at the end of 12 months it is no longer possible for the gift to be defeated, then the exemption is allowed with the defeasance provisions deleted. For example, if there is a gift to a charity with a gift over if the charity changes its name, if the charity has not changed its name within 12 months of the transfer, then the charity will take absolutely and the gift over be deleted; or

(d) if the property given is an interest in other property, that interest must not be less than the donor's. This question is decided 12 months after the date of the transfer; or

(e) the property is given for a limited period; or

(f) if the property is land or a building and given subject to an interest reserved or created by the donor which entitles him, his spouse or a person connected with him to possession of, or to occupy, the whole or any part of the land or building rent free or at a rent less than might be expected to be obtained in a transaction at arm's length between persons not connected with each other. Once again this question is decided 12 months after the date of the transfer; or

(g) if the property is not land or a building and is given subject to an interest reserved or created by the donor other than one which is created by him for full consideration in money or money's worth or is an interest which does not substantially affect the enjoyment of the property by the person or body to whom it is given. Once again, this question is decided 12 months after the date of the transfer; or

(h)   if the property given or any part of it may become applicable for purposes other than charitable purposes or for a political party or for national purposes or for public benefit.

Gifts to political parties (s 24)

5.13   Any gift to a qualifying political party is exempt without limit if made more than one year from the date of death, but otherwise the exemption is restricted to £100,000.

Qualifying political party

5.14   A qualifying political party is one where at the last General Election preceding the transfer either two members of that party were elected to the House of Commons or one member of that party was elected and not less than 150,000 votes were given to candidates who were members of that party.

Conditions

5.15   Exactly the same conditions applying to charities (para **5.12** above) are also imposed on this exemption.

Gifts for national purposes, etc (s 25)

5.16   Gifts to any one or more of 19 bodies and institutions specified in Sch 3 of the 1984 Act are exempt without limit. These bodies comprise the National Gallery, the British Museum, the Royal Scottish Museum, the National Museum of Wales, the Ulster Museum, any Treasury-approved similar national institution, any museum or art gallery maintained by a local authority or university in the UK, university teaching or research libraries in the UK, the Historic Buildings and Monuments Commission, the National Trust, the National Trust for Scotland, the National Art Collections Fund, the Trustees of the National Heritage Memorial Fund, the Friends of the National Libraries, the Historic Churches Preservation Trust, the Nature Conservancy Council, any local authority, any government department and any university or university college in the UK.

Conditions

5.17   There is no limit on the exemption whether made as a lifetime gift or on death, but exactly the same conditions apply as in the case of charities (para **5.12**) with the exception of the last condition which will not be breached in relation to property consisting of the benefit of an agreement restricting the use of land.

Gifts for public benefit (s 26)

5.18 An exemption without limit on the amount given also extends to gifts made to a body not established or conducted for profit provided the Treasury directs before or after the gift that the exemption is to be available. The property to which this exemption applies is set out in s 26(2) of the Act as follows:

(a)   land which in the opinion of the Treasury is of outstanding scenic or historic or scientific interest;

(b)   a building for the preservation of which special steps should in the opinion of the Treasury be taken by reason of its outstanding historic or architectural or aesthetic interest and the cost of preserving it;

(c)   land used as the grounds of a building within para (b) above;

(d)   an object which at the time of the transfer is ordinarily kept in, and which is given with, a building within para (b) above;

(e)   property given as a source of income for the upkeep of property within any of the paragraphs of this sub-section;

(f)   a picture, print, book, manuscript, work of art or scientific collection which in the opinion of the Treasury is of national, scientific, historic or artistic interest.

Conditions

5.19 Exactly the same conditions apply as in the case of charities (para **5.12** above). Further the Treasury must consider the body is an appropriate one and that the income from the property is not more than necessary for the upkeep of the property (with a reasonable margin). Further, the Treasury may require undertakings restricting the use or disposal of the property, securing the preservation of the property and reasonable access to it for the public.

EXEMPT LIFETIME TRANSFERS

5.20 This category of exemptions consists of lifetime gifts which are not to exempt transferees and would therefore normally constitute chargeable transfers, but nevertheless are exempt within the limits of the exemption given. These exemptions are available to each spouse in his or her own right, subject to the associated operations provisions (see para **1.24**).

Annual exemptions (s 19)

5.21 Transfers up to £3,000 in any tax year are exempt (£2,000 before 6 April 1981 and £1,000 before 6 April 1976). Once the annual exemption for the year has been fully utilised, then so much of the previous year's annual exemption as is still available may then be utilised. It is only possible to carry forward any shortfall for one year.

EXAMPLE
A father, who has made no previous chargeable transfers, makes a gift of £4,000 to his son in May 1985, a gift of £2,000 to his daughter in May 1986 and a gift of £6,000 to his grandson in May 1987. The gift to the son will be exempt by utilising the annual exemption for that year of £3,000 and £1,000 from the previous year, there having been no previous transfer. The gift to the daughter will be exempt as it is under the limit of the exemption and there will be available a carry forward of £1,000. The gift to the grandson will be exempt to the extent of the annual exemption of £3,000 plus the £1,000 carried forward from the previous year, but the balance of the gift of £2,000 will be chargeable.

5.22 The annual exemption is not available on death, except that under s 57, it may be used if there is a termination of an interest in possession under a settlement, provided notification is given to the trustees within six months of the date of the death.

Small gifts exemption (s 20)

5.23 Gifts of not more than £250 each may be given to an unlimited number of persons in any one tax year, provided no one receives more than £250 from the transferor, which prevents the availability of this exemption in addition to the annual exemption to the same person. This exemption is not available on death nor on the termination of an interest in possession under s 57.

Gifts in consideration of marriage (s 22)

The consideration of marriage

5.24 Gifts made in consideration of marriage are exempt within certain limits, depending on the relationship between the parties. To qualify under this head, a gift must be made in consideration of marriage. A gift is not treated as being in consideration of marriage unless it is made before or contemporaneously with the marriage, or afterwards in pursuance of an agreement made before or contemporaneously with the marriage. If a gift is made merely on the occasion of the marriage or made conditionally on the marriage taking place it is not necessarily made in consideration of the marriage; it is a question of fact in each case.

Limits of exemption

5.25 The limits of this exemption are as follows:

(a) the first £5,000 of the gift made in consideration of marriage by the parent of either party to the marriage. Effectively this means that four parents can between them make exempt transfers of £20,000 to the married couple;

(b) where the transferor is a remoter ancestor or is a party to the marriage (this only being relevant if the transferee is domiciled abroad), the first £2,500 is exempt;

(c) the first £1,000 of a marriage gift made by any other person.

Settled gifts

5.26 There are no restrictions placed on these exemptions where the gift is an outright gift direct to the couple, but where the gift is by way of settlement, the exemptions of £5,000 and £2,500 only apply if the settlement is primarily for the benefit of the parties to the marriage, their issue (including those legitimated by the marriage or adopted by the parties to the marriage) and the spouses of such issue. If these conditions are not met then the exemption is limited to £1,000.

Normal expenditure out of income (s 21)

Definition

5.27 This is another exemption which has been carried down from the estate duty. A transfer is exempt to the extent that it is shown that:

(a) it was made as part of the normal expenditure of the transferor; and

(b) that taking one year with another it was made out of income; and

(c) that after allowing for all transfers forming part of his expenditure, the transferor was left with sufficient net income to maintain his usual standard of living.

Only excess expenditure disallowed

5.28 This modifies the old estate duty exemption in an important respect. Under the estate duty provisions, if the expenditure was considered in excess of normal expenditure out of income, then the whole exemption was lost, but now it is provided that when the transfer exceeds the normal expenditure limit, only the excess is chargeable.

Purchased life annuities

5.29 The old estate duty exemption is also modified in another respect as it is now provided that the capital repayment element in a purchased life annuity is not treated as part of the transferor's income for this purpose if purchased after 12 November 1974.

Normal pattern of expenditure

5.30 Whether a gift forms part of the transferor's normal expenditure is a question of fact. A normal pattern of expenditure will assist in establishing this exemption, such as payment of premiums on life policies taken out for the benefit of children or payments made under a deed of covenant.

Conditionally exempt transfers (ss 30–35)

5.31 Certain transfers, whether made during a lifetime (subject to certain period of ownership qualifications) or on death, may be granted conditional exemption from inheritance tax if the assets involved are of national importance and subject to certain undertakings being given. Where such conditional exemption is given, no tax is paid on the transfer, but tax may be recovered if the condition is breached.

Chargeable events

5.32 The detailed provisions are set out in ss 30–35, including the assets which qualify (s 31) and the chargeable events which will remove the exemption, such as breach of undertaking, sale of the assets or a gift of the assets (s 32). Detailed provisions are also laid down under s 33 as to how the tax is calculated on the occurrence of a chargeable event, including reinstatement of the transferor's cumulative total (s 34).

Death on active service (s 154)

5.33 This exemption, which is only available on death, is considered at para **4.14**.

Voidable transfers (s 150)

5.34 In certain circumstances a transfer may be declared voidable, such as where it was made with intent to defraud creditors or in certain cases on the subsequent bankruptcy of the transferor or where there has been undue influence. In the event of such a transfer being declared void, it is deemed to have been void ab initio and any tax repaid accordingly; it may also necessitate a re-assessment of subsequent transfers and adjustment to the cumulative total. This may arise, for example, where an elderly person makes a gift to her professional adviser under undue influence and then the transferee has the gift set aside. The gift is treated as though it had never been made, both from the point of view of cumulation and of repayment of any tax.

Abolition of exemption in respect of mutual transfers

5.35 This exemption, formerly available under ss 148 and 149, provided that a gift back by the donee to the donor was, subject to certain restrictions, totally exempt if made within 12 months of the original transfer, and proportionately reduced for each full period of 12 months thereafter. This exemption has now been abolished in respect of any transfer back made after 17 March 1986 (FA 1986, Sch 19, para 25).

CHAPTER 6

Valuation

Introduction

6.01 Inheritance tax is a tax on a transfer of value, the amount of which is the loss to the transferor's estate which, as already illustrated at para **1.12**, is not necessarily the same as the value of the asset transferred. However, in the majority of situations it will be necessary to value the loss to the transferor's estate by reference to the value of the assets disposed of.

The basic rule (s 160)

6.02 The basic rule of valuation for inheritance tax purposes is contained in s 160 which provides that

'the value at any time of any property shall for the purposes of (inheritance tax) be the price which the property might reasonably be expected to fetch if sold in the open market at that time; but that price shall not be assumed to be reduced on the ground that the whole property is placed on the market at one and the same time'.

This rule is the same as that applied to capital gains tax and used to be applied to estate duty.

6.03 As no allowance is made for the fact that the whole property is put on the market at the same time, this effectively means that a higher value may be placed on the property for tax purposes than if it were actually sold on the open market. So, for example, if a farmer has three farms, the fact that putting them all on the market at the same time might depress the price does not reduce their value for tax purposes and each one is valued disregarding the existence of the other two.

Sale of land within three years (s 191)

6.04 This rule, however, may sometimes be mitigated by the relief given under s 191, substituting the sale price for the probate value if land is sold within three years of death (see para **4.38**).

6.05 *Valuation*

Relief where value falls before death (s 131)

6.05 Under s 131, where tax becomes payable on a potentially exempt transfer, or additional tax becomes payable on a lifetime chargeable transfer, in the event of the death of the transferor within seven years of the transfer, if the transferee or his spouse has retained or sold the property, the sale price may be substituted, subject to certain conditions (see para **4.06**)

The special purchaser

6.06 On the other hand, the fact that there is a special purchaser for a particular property may nevertheless be taken into account. Accordingly, if the transferor owns a parcel of land which two adjoining owners are especially anxious to acquire, the fact that they would pay above the market price will be a factor to be taken into consideration, although the value will not necessarily be the ultimate market price that would be paid for the land. This is not contrary to the normal rule of valuation, but merely a method of endeavouring to find the market value according to the particular asset being valued if it were put on the open market, such as offered by auction.

6.07 The situation of a special purchaser may arise in the case of a private company where the shareholders may be particularly anxious to acquire the transferor's shares to prevent them going elsewhere. While this factor will be taken into consideration, so will the existence of any restriction on the sale, such as the usual pre-emption clauses contained in the articles of association of private companies.

Restrictions on transfer (s 163)

6.08 The rule that a restriction on the transfer of an asset must be taken into account when arriving at its value cannot be used as a means of avoidance, such as by the transferor imposing a restriction on the property so as to reduce its value and subsequently making a transfer of value of the property subject to the restriction. Where by a contract made at any time, an exclusion or restriction has been imposed on the right to dispose of any property, then on the occasion of the next chargeable transfer of that property, that exclusion or restriction is to be taken into account only to the extent (if any) that consideration of money or money's worth was given for it. However, if the contract was a chargeable transfer or part of associated operations which together were a chargeable transfer, an allowance is made for the reduction in value.

EXAMPLE
A father agrees with his son to grant an option to purchase the father's property at £50,000 at any time during the next five years. The son pays the full market value of the option of £5,000. The son then exercises the option in five years' time when the value of the property has risen to £100,000.

On the sale to the son, the option is disregarded and the father will be deemed to have made a transfer of value of £45,000 (£100,000 – [£50,000 + £5,000]).

6.09 If the next transfer is not a chargeable transfer, the restriction will be taken into account on the next subsequent chargeable transfer which therefore avoids the possibility of passing a property through an exempt transferee (such as a spouse) before making the ultimate gift.

6.10 Where the contract was made before 27 March 1974, this rule only applies if the next chargeable transfer was on death.

Sales on the open market

6.11 If the property is sold on the open market after the transfer, this provides some evidence of the value if the sale takes place reasonably soon. This, however, is assuming that there are no other factors intervening between the date of the transfer and the date of the sale. For example, when the property is transferred it may be subject to a protected tenancy, but if at the time it is sold it is with vacant possession, then the value will normally be substantially higher.

6.12 If the property is sold then once again the provisions of ss 191 and 131 may be relevant for substituting the sale price as mentioned in para **6.04** and **6.05** above.

RELATED PROPERTY (s 161)

6.13 Normally a transferor's estate is valued without reference to any assets owned by other persons. If this rule was always applied, the value of an asset could be substantially reduced by first utilising an exemption to reduce its value.

6.14 Utilising the exemptions in this way in many cases may well be caught by the associated operations provisions (considered in para **1.24**), but this would not always necessarily be so.

6.15 *Valuation*

EXAMPLE

If a father holds a 51% shareholding in a close company and his son owns a 49% shareholding, on the father's death the loss to his estate would be substantially more than a 51% share in the company as his holding represents control of the company. Even if the father were to give his son 2%, the loss to his estate would again be substantial because that 2% would represent the loss of control in the company. If, however, the father gave a 2% shareholding to, say, a charity, then that disposition would itself be exempt. On the father's death, perhaps many years later, it may be difficult to prove an associated operation; he could leave his son a 49% minority shareholding in the company.

6.15   As an anti-avoidance device, therefore, the related property rules provide that, contrary to the normal rule, the value of the transferor's assets are not considered in isolation, but together with other assets constituting related property.

6.16   These rules only operate if the value of the transferor's assets are increased and do not operate to reduce the value.

Definition (s 161)

6.17   It is provided in s 161 that a person's property is related if:

(a)   it is comprised in the estate of his spouse; or
(b)   it is property which has within the preceding five years been the property of a charity or held in trust for charitable purposes only or been the property of an exempt body and became so on the transfer of value made by either spouse after 15 April 1976 and was exempt to the extent that the value transferred was attributable to the property.

6.18   Prior to 10 March 1981, property comprised in a discretionary settlement was also related with property comprised in the transferor's estate if the discretionary settlement had been created by the deceased or his spouse. This particular provision was removed by the FA 1981, s 105.

Consequences

6.19   Where these provisions apply, a total valuation is arrived at of the transferor's assets aggregated with the related property. Having established this total valuation, the value of the transferor's assets is then taken to be pro rata to his share of the aggregated value.

EXAMPLE 1

A husband and wife each own a Ming vase which individually are worth £50,000, but as a pair are worth £200,000. If the husband were then to give away one of the vases, under these provisions, the loss to his estate would not be £50,000 but one-half of the total value of his own property and that of his wife's to which it is related, which in the present example would be half of £200,000, which would therefore represent the loss to the husband's estate.

EXAMPLE 2

A husband and wife each own 30% of the shares in a company. The value of a 30% shareholding in the company is £30,000. But for the related property provisions, if the husband were to give away his shareholding to his son, then the loss to his estate would be £30,000. However, the related property provisions provide that the assets of the spouses are added together to arrive at a total value. In the present example a 60% holding giving control of the company may be worth £120,000. If that was so, then the loss to the husband's estate would then be deemed to be half of £120,000 and not the actual value of £30,000.

Interaction with business property relief

6.20　If these provisions apply and an aggregated figure is arrived at, then when considering business property relief, it is also assumed that the full value was held by the transferor. So in Example 2 above, where both spouses each had a 30% shareholding in the company, although for the purpose of valuation the husband was deemed to have half of a 60% holding, he is also deemed to have control of the company and it will therefore attract 50% business relief rather than a mere 30% as a minority shareholder.

Extension to property held on trust

6.21　The property of the transferor's spouse which is related to the property of the transferor applies to all assets in which the spouse has a beneficial interest in possession, as s 49(1) provides that a person beneficially entitled to an interest in possession in settled property shall be treated as beneficially entitled to the property in which the interest subsists. This would mean that if a husband had a 49% shareholding in his own right in a company and his wife had a life interest in a 11% holding, then, for the purpose of the related property provisions, the husband's holding would be valued at a proportion of a 60% shareholding.

6.22 The related property rule is an anti-avoidance provision to prevent an intending donor diminishing the value of his estate by using an exemption and then proceeding to take a transfer of the asset which is diminished in value. Being an anti-avoidance provision, it may work unfairly as the source of the assets is irrelevant; it arises from the relationship of the parties and not the source of the asset. If, therefore, spouses have totally independently acquired assets which are treated as related, possibly even before they were married or each purchased independently before or during the marriage, nevertheless these provisions will apply.

Relief if sold within three years of death (s 176)

6.23 To some extent the severity of these provisions may be relieved, by virtue of s 176, where there is a qualifying sale within three years of the death of a person in whose estate was comprised property valued by reference to related property which realises less than the valuation on death. This relief enables the property to be valued without reference to the related property.

Qualifying sale

6.24 A qualifying sale is one which satisfies all the following conditions:

(a) the vendors are either the persons in whom the property was vested immediately after death or are the deceased's personal representatives;

(b) the sale is at arm's length for a price freely negotiated at the time of the sale independent of any sale of the property to which it is related;

(c) the vendor and purchaser are unconnected; and

(d) neither the vendors nor any other person having an interest in the proceeds of sale obtain in connection with this sale a right to acquire the property sold or any interest in it.

The relief

6.25 The relief given does not substitute the lower sale price. Where the sale price is lower than the value calculated by reference to related property, it allows the asset to be valued isolated from the related property rules.

6.26 The relief is only available if the sale price is less than the value (ascertained by reference to related property) placed on the property on death.

6.27   The relief must be claimed. It may not always be advisable to make a claim if, for example, the asset re-valued in isolation will reduce the amount of business property relief available (see para **6.20**).

6.28   The relief given under s 176 is, of course, independent of any relief that may be claimed in respect of sale of qualifying shares within 12 months of death (see para **4.32**) or the sale of land within three years of death (see para **4.38**).

Jointly-owned property

6.29   Where property is jointly owned, then each individual share of the co-owners may be discounted between 10% and 15%, depending on the particular circumstances, to allow for the fact that it is more difficult to sell a share in, rather than the whole of, an asset.

6.30   This may work to the taxpayer's advantage where the transferor only has a share in property which is therefore suitably discounted before ascertaining the loss to his estate. However, where property is jointly owned by spouses and one of the spouses gives away his or her share of the property, it is not discounted because of the related property rules which provide that on any transfer each spouse is deemed to transfer a proportionate part of the value of the whole.

6.31   Furthermore, if the transferor owns the whole of the property and gives away a share in it, this has the effect of increasing the loss to his estate for now he only has a share in the property which must be discounted in value before arriving at the net loss to his estate.

Valuation of debts due to the estate (s 166)

6.32   Any moneys due to the transferor's or a deceased's estate will form part of the estate except if and to the extent that recovery of the sum is impossible or not reasonably practical and has not become so by any act or omission of the person to whom the sum is due (see para **4.20**).

VALUATION OF LIABILITIES

6.33   As it is the net loss to the transferor's estate which represents the transfer of value, when a person incurs a liability then the value of his estate is reduced. On death, a person is deemed to have made a transfer of value of the whole of his estate and therefore when valuing the estate the liabilities are generally to be taken into account unless they have been created voluntarily or artificially to reduce the value of the estate.

Liability incurred by the transferor (s 5(5))

6.34   A liability of the estate is normally deductible from its value provided (except in the case of a liability imposed by law) it was incurred for a consideration in money or money's worth.

Debts created voluntarily

6.35   Consequently, if a person creates a voluntary liability of his estate, such as a covenant, which is undischarged when he dies, it will be disallowed as a liability in assessing the net value of the estate and this will apply even if there is a consideration, other than a consideration in money or money's worth, such as a covenant by a parent for his child's marriage settlement.

Inflated debts

6.36   Further, as the deduction is only allowed to the extent it was incurred for a consideration in money or money's worth, if a debt has been incurred in excess of the consideration given in exchange, such as an agreement to purchase an asset at an over value, the debt is not deductible to the extent that consideration was not given. As an example, if a father buys a car worth £2,000 from his son at £5,000 and the father dies without having paid for it at the date of his death, the debt is only deductible to the extent of £2,000.

'Artificial' debts (FA 1986, s 103)

6.37   The provisions just outlined above have not been totally superseded by the new restrictions imposed by the FA 1986, s 103. These new rules are an extension of the restriction on the deductibility of debts from a deceased person's estate on death for tax purposes where debts or encumbrances have been incurred or created by the deceased.

6.38   These new restrictions only apply to debts and encumbrances incurred or created after 17 March 1986 and are a revival of the estate duty provisions restricting the deductibility of debts which are artificially created by the deceased.

Debts disallowed to extent derived from the deceased

6.39 A debt incurred or encumbrance created is disallowed to the extent to which the consideration for it is property derived from the deceased, or to the extent that is given by a person whom the deceased directly or indirectly put in funds for the purpose (FA 1986, s 103(1)–(3)). As an illustration, if a father with a view to reducing inheritance tax on his death gives his property to his son but wishes to retain the income and control during his lifetime, he could gift the property to his son and then buy it back at a full market consideration, leaving the purchase price unpaid. On the father's death, the property would be taxable (as indeed it would if he had reserved a benefit in it) but the purchase price would be a deduction from his estate, but for the provisions of s 103.

6.40 To qualify as a deduction, the creation (which includes by associated operations) of such debts and liabilities must not constitute a transfer of value and must have been incurred or created for full consideration in money or money's worth paid to the deceased for his own use or benefit. Otherwise such debts will abate to the extent that the consideration derived from the deceased or came from someone who had directly or indirectly received the property from the deceased.

Repayment treated as a potentially exempt transfer (FA 1986, s 103(5)).

6.41 To the extent that the liability is discharged by the person incurring the liability before his death and after 17 March 1986, any money or money's worth paid or applied towards satisfaction of the debt will not be treated as in satisfaction of the debt, but it will be treated as a potentially exempt transfer equal to the money or money's worth so paid or applied towards satisfaction of the debt.

Illustration

6.42 These provisions can be illustrated with an example:

EXAMPLE

A father gives Blackacre to his son in August 1986 and in September 1986 the son sells the property to his father for its current market value of £50,000. The father pays no money but the consideration is treated as a loan by the son to the father.

In October 1990 the father repays his son £36,000. The father dies in December 1992.

The debt incurred by the father in 1986 is not deductible from his estate, but to the extent the £30,000 was repaid in 1990, it is treated as a potentially exempt transfer.

When the father dies in 1992, the balance of the debt due to the son of £20,000 will not be an allowable deduction and the £30,000 which the father repaid his son in 1990 will be treated as a potentially exempt transfer, but as the father died within three years the tax thereon (if any) will be paid at the full rate and of course the transfer cumulated with any subsequent transfers and with his estate.

Liability incurred by a life insurance policy (FA 1986, s 103(7))

6.43 A liability relating to a life insurance policy issued after 30 June 1986 is disallowed unless the full proceeds of that policy form part of the estate on death. This would therefore, for example, preclude an arrangement with an insurance company that in return for a payment to be made out of the estate on death, the insurance company makes a payment to a beneficiary of the deceased's choice.

Other debts

6.44 In the case of debts which are not incurred by the transferor himself, but which he has an obligation to pay, these are also deductible. This may arise, for example, if he receives property subject to a mortgage or subject to payment of inheritance tax which are therefore deductible in arriving at the net value of the asset.

Debts which are not deductible

6.45 A debt is not deductible to the extent that neither the personal representative nor anyone else is liable to pay the debt, nor is it charged on any property. This is illustrated by the decision of *Re Barnes*. The deceased made lifetime gifts which had attracted estate duty of £185,000 as he had died within the statutory period. The assets in his estate comprised £12 and the debts and funeral expenses amounted to £95,000. It was held that estate duty was payable on the value of the lifetime gifts without being able to deduct the debts and funeral expenses, as those liabilities were neither chargeable on the gifts nor payable by the donees. It was irrelevant that the donees had in fact accepted a moral obligation and paid the debts.

Debts not enforceable by law

6.46 Similarly, debts which are not enforceable by law, such as gaming debts, debts under illegal contracts, or debts required to be evidenced in writing to be enforceable, are not deductible debts. Conversely, if these debts are 'due' to the estate they do not form part of the estate.

6.47 A debt is not deductible to the extent that there is a right to reimbursement. This may arise where the deceased has been a tenant under a lease which is assigned in his lifetime. On his death a landlord may have a claim against the estate as the deceased was the original tenant, but such a debt would not be allowable unless the personal representatives are unable to obtain payment against the indemnity given by the assignee of the lease.

6.48 Debts or liabilities incurred by the personal representatives, such as administration expenses or debts incurred by beneficiaries, such as the cost of a headstone, are not liabilities of the deceased and are therefore not deductible in calculating the value of his estate immediately before his death. Funeral expenses are expressly allowed as a debt of the estate (s 172) as are many expenses incurred (but not exceeding 5%) in connection with administering or realising property situate outside the UK (s 173).

Debts charged on property (s 162(4))

6.49 A liability which is an encumbrance on any property shall, so far as possible, be taken to reduce the value of that property. This is of particular importance where the deduction of the encumbrance will reduce the value of an exemption or relief. Accordingly, if a husband leaves the matrimonial home, which is subject to a building society mortgage, to his widow, the transfer to the widow will be exempt and the debt to the building society reduces the value of the property transferred and will not be taken into account in calculating the net value of the remainder of the estate unless the actual debt exceeds the value of the asset on which it is charged.

6.50 However, it should be borne in mind that in the absence of contrary provision in the will, where there is a charged debt on a gifted asset, the burden of discharging that debt is borne by the beneficiary of that asset. If in the last illustration there had been a legacy to the widow of an amount equivalent to the building society mortgage, then, of course, the spouse exemption would be given on that legacy.

Debts charged on more than one property

6.51 Where a debt is charged on a number of assets, the person liable to pay the debt can select on which item to claim the deduction.

So if the deceased's mortgage was on his matrimonial home which he left to his widow, and a town house which he left to his daughter, his personal representatives could elect on which asset the debt should be deducted.

Debts charged on property qualifying for relief

6.52 In the case of business property relief and agricultural property relief, where a debt is an encumbrance on any property, it is first deducted from the value of the property before arriving at the relief and will therefore reduce the value of the relief which it would not have done if it had been a general debt of the estate (see paras **7.23** and **7.65** respectively).

Foreign liabilities (s 162(5))

6.53 Where there is a liability to a person resident outside the UK, it is a deductible debt, but if the liability falls to be discharged outside the UK and it is not an encumbrance on the property inside the UK, the liability is, so far as possible, to be taken to reduce the value of the property outside the UK. The purpose of this is that if a person is domiciled outside the UK he is only liable to capital transfer tax on property inside the UK and he is therefore prevented from deducting all his overseas debts from the UK assets.

Tax liability arising from the transfer (s 5(4) and s 162(3))

6.54 The transferor's liability to inheritance tax resulting from the transfer is taken into account in determining the value of his estate immediately after the transfer. This is the basis of the grossing-up rule as the loss to the transferor's estate is the total of what he has transferred and the tax he has to pay (see para **3.13**). The liability of any other tax, however, is not taken into account such as where the transferor becomes liable for capital gains tax, although should he die before paying the capital gains tax then, of course, it will be a debt of his estate in the usual way.

CHAPTER 7

Reliefs

Introduction

7.01 There are two categories of assets, business property and agricultural property, which receive favourable treatment by the reduction of the chargeable value of the asset, whether the transfer is made in a person's lifetime or on death. This has the advantage of reducing the tax burden on the whole estate, not merely on the relieved property, as it reduces the total chargeable value of the estate. To avoid abuse of these substantial reliefs, strict requirements have to be complied with. The rates of relief now applying in the case of business property were different before 15 March 1983. In the case of agricultural property relief, the rules to qualify for relief were totally changed by the FA 1981 in respect of transfers after 9 March 1981, and at the same time a lower rate of relief was introduced if the transferor was not in possession or did not have the right to obtain it within 12 months of the transfer. The FA 1986 has amended the method of allocating these reliefs and imposed ownership conditions on the transferee, as outlined later in this chapter.

BUSINESS PROPERTY RELIEF (ss 103–114)

7.02 To qualify for this relief, the property must be 'relevant business property' *and* must have been owned by the transferor for the period of two years immediately preceding the transfer. The relief is given by reducing the value of the asset by 50% or 30% depending on the nature of the asset involved.

Qualifying relevant business property

7.03 Under s 105(1) the following assets qualify as relevant business property:

(a) the business of a sole proprietor or the interest of a partner in a business;

(b) quoted or unquoted shares in or securities of a trading company controlled by the transferor immediately before the transfer;

(c) a minority holding of unquoted shares in a trading company;
(d) any land or building, machinery or plant which, immediately before the transfer, was used wholly or mainly for the purpose of a business carried on by a company of which the transferor then had control or by a partnership of which he was then a partner; and
(e) any land or building, machinery or plant which, immediately before the transfer, was used wholly or mainly by a trading company for the purpose of a business carried on by the transferor and was settled property in which he was then beneficially entitled to an interest in possession.

The relief given

7.04　The relief given is to reduce the relevant business asset by 50% in the case of categories (a) and (b) and by 30% in all other cases.

Businesses not qualifying for relief (s 105(3)–(7))

7.05　Businesses consisting wholly or mainly of one of the following do *not* qualify for relief:

(a) those dealing in securities, stocks or shares (except for the business of a market maker or discount house carried on in the UK, as now defined by s 105(7) (inserted by the FA 1986, s 106(2)).
(b) those dealing in land or buildings, although this would not normally preclude relief to a builder who deals in land and buildings, and which dealing is ancillary to his main business of construction;
(c) those making or holding investments (unless of a company wholly or mainly holding shares in a company which qualifies for relief).

7.06　Further, shares in or securities of a company do not qualify if at the time of the transfer the company is in the process of liquidation (except for a reconstruction or amalgamation effected for carrying on the business).

7.07　Relief is only available on assets which are used wholly or mainly for the purpose of the business throughout the two years immediately preceding the transfer or are needed for future use by the business (s 112(2)).

Ownership qualification (ss 107–109)

7.08 To qualify for relief, the property must be owned by the transferor throughout the period of two years immediately preceding the transfer.

Replacement properties (s 107)

7.09 The property will also qualify if it has replaced other qualifying business property which was owned by the transferor for at least two years in the five years immediately preceding the transfer. However, in this case the value qualifying for relief is the lower of either the property replaced or the value of the transfer (except this lower value does not apply if it is a result of the formation, alteration or dissolution of a partnership or from the acquisition of a business by a company controlled by the former owner of the business.)

Successions (s 108)

7.10 If the transferor became entitled to the property on a death he is deemed to have owned it from the date of that death and if the deceased was his spouse he is also deemed to have owned it for any period during which the spouse owned it.

EXAMPLE
A husband, who has owned business property for one year, dies, leaving it to his wife. If the wife now survives her husband by a further year, the wife will be deemed to have owned the property for two years, if she were now to make a transfer of value.

This provision only applies where the spouse succeeds on death and would not apply in this illustration if the husband had made a lifetime gift to his wife. This is particularly important to bear in mind where the life expectancy of the donee is short and would have to qualify in his or her own right for the full period of two years.

Successive transfers (s 109)

7.11 The property will also qualify if it has been acquired on a qualifying transfer of value even if the present transferor has not owned it for two years, provided the previous transfer *or* the present transfer is on death.

EXAMPLE
A father who has owned business property for over two years makes a lifetime gift to his son, who is killed a year later. The business property in the son's estate will qualify for relief.
Relief would not have been available if the father had owned the

business for only 18 months, as he would not then have qualified at the time of the transfer. Nor would relief have been available if the son had made a lifetime gift, as then neither transfers would have been on death.

Retention of ownership by transferee qualification (ss 113A and 113B, inserted by the FA 1986, Sch 19, para 21)

7.12 In respect of *all* lifetime transfers made after 17 March 1986, where the death of the transferor occurs within seven years of the date of the transfer, further conditions on the part of the transferee have to be observed before business property relief can be claimed on the property transferred. *Both* the following conditions must be satisfied:

(a)   the original property transferred must have continued to be owned by the transferee from the date of the transfer up to the date of death of the transferor; *and*

(b)   the property must have continued to have been relevant business property up to the date of death of the transferor.

If the transferee has predeceased the transferor, these conditions will be met if they are satisfied at the date of death of the transferee.

If only part of the property transferred satisfies these conditions, only that part of the property will qualify for the relief.

Continuing qualifying business ownership up to death

7.13 If the transferor dies within seven years of any lifetime transfer made after 17 March 1986, these further restrictions therefore now require that the business property (or the replacement property as mentioned below) must continue to be owned by the transferee up to the date of the transferor's death (or earlier death of the transferee) and not only must the property (or the replacement property) qualify for business relief at the time of the transfer, but continue to qualify up to the date of death of the transferor (or earlier death of the transferee). The relief would therefore be lost if the transferee disposed of the property by way of sale (subject to the replacement provisions mentioned below) or gift in the event of the transferor dying within the seven years.

Replacement shares (s 113A (6))

7.14 Where the transferee owns shares immediately before the date of death of the transferor (or earlier death of the transferee) which:

(a)   would under any of the provisions of ss 77 to 86 of the Capital

Gains Tax Act 1979 be identified with the original property (or part of it), or

(b) were issued to him in consideration of the transfer of a business or interest in a business consisting of the original property (or part of it),

the shares shall be treated as if they were the original property (or that part of it).

Replacement properties (s 113B)

7.15 Where the transferee has disposed of the whole or part of the original property transferred (which includes replacement shares as described in para **7.14** above) before the death of the transferor and the whole consideration has been applied by him in acquiring a replacement property, the replacement property will continue to qualify for business property relief provided all the following conditions are satisfied:

(a) the replacement property is acquired within 12 months of the disposal;

(b) the disposal and acquisition are both made in transactions at arm's length or on terms such as might be expected to be included in a transaction at arm's length;

(c) the *whole* of the consideration for the disposal is applied in acquiring a replacement property;

(d) the replacement property is owned by the transferee immediately before the death of the transferor;

(e) throughout the period from the date of the original transfer and ending with the death (apart from the 12 months permitted for replacement), either the original or the replacement property was owned by the transferee;

(f) the replacement property qualifies as relevant business property immediately before the death.

If the transferee has predeceased the transferor, any conditions required to be satisfied at the date of death of the transferor will be met if they are satisfied at the date of death of the transferee.

If the transferor dies before the transferee, but the transferee has disposed of the original property before the date of death of the transferor, he may acquire replacement property within 12 months of the disposal of the original property. The replacement property will qualify for relief without having to comply with (d) above, and any reference to a time immediately before the death of the transferor is deemed to be a reference to the time when the replacement property is acquired, but otherwise the last two conditions must be met at the time the replacement property is acquired (s 113B(5)).

Reassessments

7.16 In the event of business property relief being lost by virtue of these provisions, not only may it result in an increase in tax payable by the transferee, but it may also necessitate a total recalculation of tax on subsequent transfers of value and on the estate.

EXAMPLE

In August 1986, a father gives to his son his garage business valued at £1,000,000 and on which business property relief is available at 50%. In May 1987, the father transfers £70,000 into an interest in possession trust. In August 1988, under pressure from his bank, the son is forced to sell the garage business. The father dies in September 1989. Assuming there have been no previous transfers and ignoring the annual relief, the tax would be ascertained as follows:

The gift to the son is a potentially exempt transfer and as such would not attract tax in August 1986.

The gift into trust would not attract tax as it falls within the nil band.

On the father's death, however, the tax would have to be re-assessed on the following basis (ignoring the annual reliefs).

The gift to the son would attract tax on £1,000,000 according to the scale applying at the date of the father's death, reduced to 80% as the death occurred between the third and fourth year.

By May 1987 the father will be deemed to have already made transfers totalling £1,000,000 and so the gift into trust will be taxed at the highest rate based on the table applying in May 1987, there being no reduction as the father died within three years of the gift.

Finally, the tax on the estate would be paid at the full marginal rate.

It will therefore be appreciated that very careful consideration will have to be given to the consequences of these new provisions coupled with the implications outlined in Chapter 2.

Contracts for sale (s 113)

7.17 If a binding contract for sale has been entered into in respect of the business property at the time of transfer, the relief is lost unless:

(a) the sale is to a company which is to carry on the business and is made in consideration wholly or mainly of shares in or securities of that company; or

(b) the property is shares in or securities of a company and the sale is made for the purpose of reconstruction or amalgamation.

Buy and sell agreements

7.18 Partnership agreements often contain provisions whereby the continuing partners have a right, or in some cases an obligation, to buy out the interest of a retiring or deceased partner, and concern has been expressed as to whether such provisions will fall within s 113 as contracts for sale.

Statement of Practice (SP12/80)

7.19 The Inland Revenue issued a Statement of Practice (SP12/80) on the 13 October 1980 with regard to such 'buy and sell' arrangements which states:

'The Inland Revenue understand that it is sometimes the practice for partners or shareholder directors of companies to enter into an agreement (known as a "Buy and Sell" Agreement) whereby, in the event of death before retirement of one of them, the deceased's personal representatives are obliged to sell and the survivors are obliged to purchase the deceased's business interest or shares, funds for the purchase being frequently provided by means of appropriate life assurance policies.

In the Inland Revenue's view such an agreement, requiring as it does a sale and purchase and not merely conferring an option to sell or buy, is a binding contract for sale within [s 113]. As a result the capital transfer tax business relief will not be due on the business interest or shares. [Section 113] provides that where any property would be relevant business property for the purpose of business relief in relation to a transfer of value but a binding contract for its sale has been entered into at the time of the transfer, it is not relevant business property in relation to that transfer'.

This Statement of Practice only extends to situations where there was an *obligation* to sell and an *obligation* to purchase, and does not therefore extend to options.

Clarification of the Statement
7.20 In view of the considerable concern aroused by this publication, the Law Society issued the following statement in *The Law Society's Gazette* (6 May 1981), referring to the Statement of Practice:

'The publication has caused a considerable amount of concern, but it is hoped that the following table will indicate that the problem is in fact far more limited than has been feared. It is hoped that practitioners will find that, in most cases, they will be able to obtain both business relief and take advantage of the instalment options for

Table 7.1

	Event	CTT payable on	Business relief available	Instalment option available
1	Partnership determines on death. Partnership assets realised and estate entitled to deceased's share of proceeds.	Value of partnership interest	Yes	Yes, until business sold.
2	Partnership continues with estate entitled to represent deceased.	Value of partnership interest	Yes	Yes.
3	Partnership continues with partnership share falling into deceased's estate but with option for other partners to aquire either on valuation or formula.	Value of partnership interest (normally calculated in accordance with valuation or formula)	Yes	Yes, until option exercised.
4	Partnership continues with share of deceased partner accruing to surviving partners with estate entitled to payment either on valuation or formula.	Value of partnership interest (normally calculated in accordance with valuation or formula).	Yes	Yes, until sums actually received from surviving partners.
5	Partnership continues and partnership share falls into deceased's estate but partnership agreement provides obligation for executors to sell and for surviving partners to buy partnership share either on valuation or in accordance with formula.	Value of partnership interest (normally calculated in accordance with valuation or formula).	No	No

CTT purposes without any significant disadvantage being caused to the partner giving away his interest or dying. It should also be mentioned that in those cases where business relief and instalment option were not available according to the drafting of the deed, it would be sensible to review the position as quickly as possible as it is thought that only in exceptional cases could there be any fear that the re-drafting of the documents would, of itself, give rise to any charge, and the business relief and instalment option availability are quite likely to be of significant benefit'. (See Table 7.1 opposite).

Accrual clauses should be reviewed

7.21 It is only in the last situation that a binding contract for sale was regarded as having come into existence before the death of a partner. Following published correspondence between the Institute of Chartered Accountants and the Inland Revenue, the Inland Revenue have stated that the intention of s 113 is to deny the relief where what the transferor passes to the transferee is in effect a right to the proceeds of sale rather than a right to a continuing business asset and that this is a matter of the wording of the partnership agreement. It does seem that the Inland Revenue are adopting a more restrictive attitude to 'accrual' clauses than indicated in *The Law Society's Gazette*. It now appears that where on the death of a partner there is provision for an accrual to the surviving partners, who are *obliged* to make a payment to the estate for the deceased partner's share, business property relief will not be available. In the case of a lifetime transfer, business property relief will be available provided the accrual provision does not actually come into operation.

Option to purchase clause

7.22 All partnership agreements containing any form of obligation to sell, such as an accrual clause under which the continuing partners are obliged to make a payment to the deceased partner's estate, must now be carefully reviewed and re-drafted, preferably as options to purchase. Such a suitable clause may be worded as follows:

'Upon the partnership being dissolved the continuing or surviving partners shall have the option of purchasing the share of the partner retiring or dying as the case may be such option being exercised in writing within six months of the date of retirement or in the case of a partner dying within 12 months of the date of death or within six months of the first grant of representation to the estate of the partner dying whichever shall be the earlier. In the event of a grant of representation to the estate of a deceased partner not being issued within six months of the date of his death the continuing partners may serve the notice to exercise the option to purchase on [the auditors] of the partnership at the date of death instead of on the personal representatives of the deceased partner. The option price shall be as agreed between the parties and in the absence of agreement is to be determined at the absolute discretion of [the auditors to the partnership at the date of dissolution or death as the case may be]'.

Valuation of business and deduction of liabilities (s 110)

Net value of business

7.23   The value of the business is its net value after deduction of any liabilities of the business. This means that any debts of the business, such as a bank overdraft or any other form of loan, are deducted from the value of the business before applying the business property relief and this applies whether or not the debts are charged on the business assets. This should be contrasted with the provisions relating to agricultural property relief, which provide that debts are not deducted from the agricultural property before applying the relief unless they are charged on the property.

Rearranging liabilities

7.24   Before making any transfer of business assets, it is, therefore, important to consider whether any liabilities of a business should be discharged before making the disposition.

EXAMPLE
A widower on his deathbed has a qualifying business worth £250,000 on which there is an overdraft of £200,000. He has a house worth £50,000 and £200,000 cash and realisable securities. If he leaves these assets to his son then the tax liability of his estate will be calculated as follows:

	£
Business	250,000
Less overdraft	200,000
	50,000
Less 50% relief	25,000
	25,000
Other assets	200,000
Chargeable estate	225,000
Tax payable	61,500

However, if before the gift he pays off the overdraft out of his cash and realisable securities, then his estate will be taxed as follows:

Business	250,000
Less relief at 50%	125,000
	125,000
Other assets (house)	50,000
Chargeable estate	175,000
Tax payable	38,050

Further, in the second situation, over 70% of the tax will qualify for payment by interest free instalments over ten years, whereas in the first situation only 11% of the tax can be postponed.

In a *deathbed* situation, if there are insufficient assets to clear a business overdraft, it would be worth considering personal borrowing to repay a business loan, possibly supported with existing life policies, which would itself be a liability of the estate and deductible from the reduced relieved value of the business property.

Inter-relation with business property relief

7.25 Where property qualifies both for agricultural property relief and for business relief, then agricultural relief must be given before business relief.

AGRICULTURAL PROPERTY RELIEF (ss 115–124)

7.26 As in the case of business property relief, the relief is given by way of a reduction in the value of the agricultural property. Where the property qualifies for business and agricultural property relief, agricultural property relief must be taken first although, of course, both reliefs cannot be given. This sometimes used to cause a problem, but now that the lower rates for both reliefs are the same (30%) this is no longer of any significance except that, in contrast to business property relief, in the case of agricultural property relief, a debt is not deducted from the value of the property before arriving at the relief unless charged on the property.

Agricultural property

7.27 Agricultural property is defined by s 115(2) as

'agricultural land or pasture and includes woodland and any buildings used in connection with the intensive rearing of livestock or fish if the woodland or building is occupied with agricultural land or pasture and the occupation is ancillary to that of the agricultural land or pasture; and also includes such cottages, farm buildings and farmhouses, together with the land occupied with them as are of a character appropriate to the property'.

The breeding and rearing of horses on a stud farm and the grazing of horses ancillary thereto is now expressly included.

The relief only extends to agricultural property in the UK, the Channel Islands or the Isle of Man.

Agricultural value

7.28 The relief only applies to the agricultural value of any agricultural property, which is defined by s 115(3) as being the value which would be the value of the property if it were subject to a perpetual covenant prohibiting its use otherwise than as agricultural property. If a higher value is attributable to the property because of its use or potential use for another purpose, then the difference between the agricultural value and the higher value does not qualify for relief. So, for example, if there is planning approval for building residential houses on agricultural land then the increase in value attributable to that planning permission does not qualify for relief. It is possible, however, that business property relief may be claimed on the difference if it qualifies on that ground.

The relief given (post–9 March 1981 rules) (s 116)

7.29 A 50% reduction in the agricultural value of the property is given if the transferor has vacant possession of the property or the right to obtain it within 12 months of the transfer. The reduction is 30% in all other cases (except prior to 15 March 1983 when this reduction was only 20%).

7.30 The interest of one or more joint tenants or tenants in common qualify for the 50% relief if the interests of all tenants together carry the right to vacant possession.

Occupation or ownership qualifications (post–9 March 1981 rules) (s 117)

Two years' occupation or seven years' ownership

7.31 To qualify for agricultural property relief, the transferor must establish one of two requirements. *Either*:

(a)   he must have occupied the property for the purpose of agriculture throughout the period of two years ending with the date of the transfer. The only requirement here is occupation for the purpose of agriculture for the requisite period, which is regardless of any period of ownership. Accordingly, a farmer who has been in possession for over two years as a tenant and who then purchases the freehold reversion can immediately make a transfer of the property and qualify for relief; *or*

(b) he must have owned the property throughout the period of seven years ending with the date of transfer and it has been occupied by himself or another throughout for agricultural purposes. This would cover, for example, a landlord who has not taken possession.

7.32 It is therefore necessary to look separately at the qualifications for relief and the requirements for the reliefs given.

Occupier not qualifying for relief

7.33 The occupier may not qualify for relief at all if he has been in occupation for less than two years and has not owned the land for seven years. He should therefore postpone any lifetime transfer until he qualifies for relief.

Landlord qualifying for 50% relief

7.34 While the principle of these rules is to give landlords relief at 30%, there are occasions when a landlord may still qualify for 50% relief. If the transferor has owned the property for seven years without having been in possession, but his interest at the time of transfer carries a right to immediate possession, then he may qualify for the maximum relief. This may arise if the landowner takes the land in hand shortly before the transfer, or has served an effective notice to quit which is to expire in less than 12 months from the date of the transfer or the transfer is made during the last 12 months of the *Gladstone v Bower* tenancy or a tenancy granted with the consent of the Ministry of Agriculture.

Vacant possession value only attracting 30% relief

7.35 Further, it is possible for the vacant possession value of the property to be applied to tenanted property so that only a 30% reduction is allowed on the vacant possession value. This could arise where the associated operations rule applies, such as where the transferor has granted a tenancy for full consideration of money or moneys worth, but has made a disposal of the reversion within three years, or has granted a tenancy for less than full consideration and made a disposal of the reversion more than three years later (see para **1.24**).

7.36 The same would apply where the related property rules operate (see para **6.13**). This would arise where a taxpayer grants a tenancy to his spouse, or in certain circumstances to a charity, and then disposes of the freehold reversion; again the basis of valuation will be at near vacant possession value, but the rate of relief will only be at 30%.

Replacement properties (s 118)

7.37 Where the property occupied by the transferor at the date of the transfer replaced other agricultural property within the five years before the transfer, then the *occupation* qualification is satisfied if the transferor occupied the properties for at least a total of two years within the five years before the transfer.

7.38 Likewise, the *ownership* qualification will be satisfied if the property transferred has replaced other agricultural property if in seven out of the last ten years before the transfer the properties have been owned by the transferor and occupied by him or another for the purpose of agriculture.

Limit on value relieved
7.39 Where these provisions apply, the value relieved shall not exceed the values of the replaced property and the new property, whichever is the lower. The relief therefore cannot be given on a value higher than the property replaced. However, replacements resulting from the formation, alteration or dissolution of a partnership can be disregarded for this purpose.

Occupation by company or partnership (s 119)

7.40 For the purpose of these provisions, occupation by a company which is controlled by the transferor is treated as occupation by the transferor so that relief is available in respect of the company's shares.

Successions (s 120)

7.41 If the transferor became entitled to the agricultural property on a death, he is deemed to have owned it (and if he subsequently occupies it, to have occupied it) from the date of that death and further if that person was his spouse then the period of occupation and ownership by the deceased's spouse can be added to that of the surviving spouse.

7.42 This provision is similar to that applying to business relief. As mentioned in para **7.10**, it is important to appreciate that the transferee spouse under a *lifetime* gift cannot utilise the periods of occupation or ownership of the transferor and will therefore have to qualify again in his or her own right.

Successive transfers (s 121)

7.43 These provisions are similar to those applying to business property (for commentary and an illustration thereon see para **7.11**). The property will qualify for relief if it has been acquired on a qualifying transfer of value even if the present transferor does not qualify in his own right, provided the previous transfer *or* the present transfer is on death *and* also provided the present transferor or his personal representative is in occupation for the purposes of agriculture. This also extends to any replacement properties.

Agricultural property of companies (ss 122, 123)

7.44 To the extent that the value of shares or securities in an agricultural company is attributable to the value of agricultural property forming part of the company's assets, they will qualify for agricultural property relief, provided those shares or securities gave the transferor control of the company. The control of the company, however, must be by virtue of shares or securities attributable to the agricultural property. Subject to these requirements, then broadly the company will qualify for relief in a similar way to individuals.

The 'working farmer' relief (where the pre–10 March 1981 rules are preserved)

7.45 When capital transfer tax was first introduced, relief was given to agricultural property on the basis of the concept of the 'working farmer'. No doubt this test was introduced to avoid the abuse of deathbed purchases of agricultural property which used to be available under the old estate duty provisions.

Conditions

7.46 The conditions for relief were contained in the FA 1975, Sch 8, whereby if a person's principal source of earned income was from farming, he would qualify for 50% relief on agricultural property of which he had possession.

7.47 Reliefs

Limits of relief

7.47 The relief was limited to agricultural property to the value of £250,000 or 1,000 acres, whichever gives the greater relief; for this purpose, rough grazing land was taken as one-sixth of its actual area.

The double discount

7.48 This relief was intended for the genuine farmer owning and occupying his own farmland. However, by taking advantage of the fact that the value of property protected by the Agricultural Holdings legislation was substantially lower than the vacant possession value of property, a 'double discount' could effectively be achieved by claiming 50% relief on the tenanted value of the agricultural property let to a partnership of which the transferor was a member. This would be achieved if there was already a tenancy of the property created before 10 March 1974 or a tenancy granted after that date at a full commercial rent and which had run for three years before making a transfer of the freehold reversion, so avoiding the associated operations provisions. In this way, after applying 50% relief the chargeable value of agricultural property would be reduced to approaching one-quarter of its full vacant possession value.

The granting of a lease as a transfer of value

7.49 There was some doubt as to whether the granting of the tenancy by the transferor to the partnership of which he was a member could itself be regarded as a transfer of value, as it effectively reduced the value of the transferor's estate. This potential difficulty was resolved by the FA 1981, s 97(1) (now s 16 of the 1984 Act) which provided there was no transfer of value by the granting of a tenancy in those circumstances.

Preservation of relief

7.50 The use of this device was prevented after 9 March 1981, but under the transitional provisions of the FA 1981, it has been preserved provided that the conditions for relief were satisfied before 10 March 1981.

7.51 Only where 50% relief of tenanted value is claimed is it relevant to consider the old provisions, as otherwise the new relief will apply, as one of the prerequisites for the old relief is that the transferor must have been in occupation.

The transitional provisions

7.52 The transitional provisions, now contained in s 116 of the 1984 Act, provide that the 50% relief on the tenanted value is available if *all* the following conditions are satisfied:

(1)   the conditions for working farmer relief were satisfied on 9 March 1981, which broadly required that

    (a)   the taxpayer should be a full-time working farmer (which is automatically evidenced if 75% of his *earned* income is derived from farming) or a person undergoing full-time education; *and*

    (b)   the transferor is in occupation (as a tenant partner or through the control of a company) of the agricultural property now transferred for the purposes of agriculture and has so occupied it for at least two years immediately preceding the transfer;

(2)   at no time between 10 March 1981 and the date of the relevant transfer was there a right to vacant possession; and

(3)   such a right has not been eliminated by any act or deliberate omission by the transferor during that period.

7.53 The relief given under these transitional provisions will be lost if the transferor ceases to be a full-time working farmer, such as, for example, should he retire before making a transfer, or if the transferor should cease to be in occupation of the agricultural property at the time he makes the transfer.

Right to vacant possession will disqualify relief

7.54 The relief will also be lost if at any time after 9 March 1981 a right to vacant possession of the property arises. This condition would be breached if the tenancy comes to an end, such as on the retirement or death of a partner, so that the tenancy and the freehold become vested in the same person or persons. Once a right to vacant possession has arisen, any subsequently created tenancy cannot benefit under the transitional provisions.

7.55 A right to vacant possession may come about by an act of the parties. So, for example, a father may own the farm, which is tenanted by himself and his son as partners under a tenancy agreement created before 10 March 1974, or after that date at a full market rental. Instead of transferring the whole of the farm into his son's name, the father may instead transfer a half share so that the property then becomes vested in the names of the son and himself. This will terminate the tenancy as the freehold reversion and the lease are now vested in the same persons. Consequently, when the father dies leaving the other half share in his will, the half share will be valued at vacant possession value.

7.56 Where this situation arises, it is suggested that the transferor should consider an assignment of the lease to more than one tenant to avoid the right to vacant possession being given inadvertently. However, when doing so, it is important to bear in mind the further requirement that such a right to vacant possession must not have been eliminated by any act or deliberate omission by the transferor after 9 March 1981. Therefore on any assignment the terms of the lease should be strictly complied with as otherwise there is a possibility that the landlord/transferor may have had grounds for forfeiting the lease, and as such omitted to act to obtain vacant possession when he had a right to do so.

Preservation of the relief on successions (s 120)

7.57 If the transferor becomes entitled to the property on the *death* of his spouse on or after 10 March 1981 and the deceased's spouse qualified for this relief, then the transferor will also qualify for relief provided neither the deceased spouse nor the transferor at any time had the right to vacant possession or failed to obtain it by any act or deliberate omission.

7.58 It is important to realise that the relief will be lost if the transferor makes a lifetime gift to his spouse such as, for example, during the process of endeavouring to equalise spouses' estates by lifetime gifts.

Retention of ownership by transferee qualification (ss 124A and 124B, inserted by the FA 1986, Sch 19, para 22)

Transferee dying within seven years of lifetime transfer

7.59 In respect of *all* lifetime transfers made after 17 March 1986, where the death of the transferor occurs within seven years of the date of the transfer, further conditions on the part of the transferee have to be observed before agricultural property relief can be claimed on the property transferred. Relief can be claimed if *all* the following conditions are satisfied:

(a) the original property transferred has continued to be owned by the transferee from the date of the transfer up to the date of death of the transferor and is not at that time subject to a binding contract of sale; *and*

(b)   (unless the case falls under (c) below) the original property is agricultural property immediately before the death and has throughout been occupied (by the transferee or another) for the purposes of agriculture since the date of the transfer to the date of death of the transferor; *and*

(c)   where the original property transferred consists of shares in, or securities of, a company, since the date of the transfer to the date of the death of the transferor, it has throughout been owned by the company and occupied (by the company or another) for the purposes of agriculture.

If the transferee has predeceased the transferor, any condition required to be satisfied at the date of death of the transferor will be met if they are satisfied at the date of death of the transferee.

If only part of a property satisfies these conditions, only that part of the property will qualify for the relief.

Continuing ownership and occupation for the purpose of agriculture

7.60   If the transferor dies within seven years of any lifetime transfer made after 17 March 1986, these further restrictions therefore now require that the agricultural property (or the replacement property as mentioned below) must continue to be owned by the transferee up to the date of the transferor's death (or earlier death of the transferee). Further, the original property (or the replacement property) must not only be agricultural property immediately before the death, but must have been occupied for the purposes of agriculture since the date of the transfer to the date of death of the transferor (or earlier death of the transferee). The relief would therefore be lost if the transferee disposes of the property by way of sale (subject to the replacement provisions mentioned below) or gift in the event of the transferor dying within the seven years.

Replacement shares (s 124A(6))

7.61   Where the transferee owns shares immediately before the date of death of the transferor (or earlier death of the transferee) which:

(a)   would under any of the provisions of ss 77 to 86 of the Capital Gains Tax Act 1979 be identified with the original property (or part of it); or

(b)   were issued to him in consideration of the transfer of agricultural property consisting of the original property (or part of it),

the shares shall be treated as if they were the original property.

Replacement properties (s 124B)

7.62   Where the transferee has disposed of the whole or part of the original property transferred (which includes replacement shares as described in **7.61** above) before the death of the transferor (or earlier death of the transferee) and the whole consideration has been applied by him in acquiring a replacement property, the replacement property will continue to qualify for agricultural property relief provided all the following conditions are satisfied:

(a)   the replacement property is acquired within 12 months of the disposal;

(b)   the disposal and acquisition are both made in transactions at arm's length or on terms such as might be expected to be included in a transaction at arm's length;

(c)   the *whole* of the consideration for the disposal is applied in acquiring a replacement property;

(d)   the replacement property is owned by the transferee immediately before the death of the transferor and is not at that time subject to a binding contract of sale;

(e)   throughout the period from the date of the original transfer to the date of disposal, the original property was owned by the transferee and occupied by him or another for the purposes of agriculture;

(f)   throughout the period from the date the transferee acquired the replacement property and ending with the death, the replacement property was owned by the transferee and occupied by him or another for the purposes of agriculture; and

(g)   the replacement property is agricultural property immediately before the death.

If the transferee has predeceased the transferor, any conditions required to be satisfied at the date of death of the transferor will be met if they are satisfied at the date of death of the transferee.

If the transferor dies before the transferee, but the transferee has disposed of the original property before the date of death of the transferor, he may acquire replacement property within 12 months of the disposal of the original property. The replacement property will qualify for relief without having to comply with (d) and (f) above, and any reference to a time immediately before the death of the transferor is deemed to be a reference to a time when the replacement property is acquired (s 124B(5)).

An exchange of agricultural land should qualify under these provisions provided there is an equality of consideration, complying with requirements (b) and (c) above.

Reassessments

7.63   In the event of agricultural property relief being lost by virtue of these provisions, not only may it result in an increase in tax payable by the transferee, but may also necessitate a total recalculation of tax on subsequent transfers of value and on the estate as illustrated in **7.16**.

Contracts for sale (s 124)

7.64   As in the case of business property, the relief is lost if at the time of the transfer there is a binding contract for the sale of the agricultural property, except where the sale is to a company and is made wholly or mainly in consideration of shares or securities in the company which gives the transferor control of it or if the sale is made for the purpose of reconstruction or amalgamation.

Charged debts

7.65   A charged debt is deducted from the value of the asset on which it is charged before applying relief, so it is only the net value which will attract valuation relief. Accordingly, if the charge on the property can be removed in advance before making a transfer, then relief will be obtained on the whole value of the agricultural property rather than the net value after deduction of the charged debt.

EXAMPLE
A father owns a farm worth £1,000,000 on which there is a mortgage of £500,000; he also has life policies and other unrelieved assets worth £500,000. If he dies leaving his entire estate to his son in that form, the chargeable estate will be arrived at as follows:

	£
Value of farm	1,000,000
Less charge	500,000
	500,000
Other assets	500,000
Chargeable estate	1,000,000

The tax will be £520,300, of which only half will qualify to be paid over ten years by interest free instalments.

If the charge on the farm was removed and the liability was unsecured or transferred to the other unrelieved assets, the calculation would therefore be as follows (on the basis that the debt would exactly cancel out the unrelieved assets):

	£
Value of farm	1,000,000
Relief at 50%	500,000
Chargeable estate	500,000

The tax would then be £300,000 less, namely £220,300, the whole of which would qualify for payment by ten interest free instalments.

Only charges on property are deducted

7.66 In the case of business relief, any liabilities of the business, whether or not charged on the business, are deducted before arriving at the net value of the business and applying the relief. In the case of agricultural property relief, no such deduction is made unless there is a charge on the property. If there is such a charge then it is deducted from the value of the property on which it is charged and it is the net value which will attract valuation relief.

Removal of charges before transfer

7.67 Consequently, if the charge on an asset is removed in advance of making a transfer, relief will be obtained on the whole value of the asset rather than the net value after deduction of the charged debt. A temporary arrangement could be made for this purpose shortly before making a lifetime transfer or in a deathbed situation.

ALLOCATION OF EXEMPTIONS (ss 36–42)

7.68 The general principles of allocation of exemptions contained in Chapter III of Pt II of the 1984 Act are considered in Chapter 10. However, by virtue of the operation of these provisions in relation to property on which there is business or agricultural relief, the tax liability could be dramatically reduced or increased depending on how the assets are disposed of in the will. These provisions have now been clarified and amended by the FA 1986 in respect of persons dying after 17 March 1986, but the previous provisions are still likely to be of some considerable importance over the two years following that date in view of the possibility of effecting a variation of the will, to maximise the benefit of these provisions, of a person dying before 18 March 1986.

Attribution of value to specific gifts

7.69 It is provided in s 38 that the value transferred, that is the value transferred after reduction by business or agricultural relief, must be attributed as far as possible to non-residuary gifts and then, by virtue of s 39, only the balance is attributed to the residue.

7.70 The effect of these provisions is that if the non-residuary gifts are made to exempt persons, these gifts can absorb the value transferred before attributing a value to the chargeable transfer.

7.71 The value transferred is therefore arrived at by first reducing the whole estate by the business or agricultural property and then attributing non-residuary gifts first. When attributing the value of the non-residuary gifts, the Inland Revenue practice was to attribute the reduced value, not the whole value, of the relieved property. A contrary view was arguable which if upheld could effectively double or halve the relief given.

The provisions applying after 17 March 1986

7.72 The Inland Revenue practice has now been adopted by virtue of s 39(A) (inserted by the FA 1986, s 105) in respect of transfers made after 17 March 1986, so that a specific gift of property attracting business or agricultural relief will be treated as reduced by the relief attributable to that property and otherwise will spread the relief rateably between exempt and non-exempt parts of the estate in accordance with a new formula.

The formula contained in s 39A(4)
7.73 It is provided by s 39(A)(2) that in respect of transfers made after 17 March 1986, where business property relief or agricultural property relief is available in the estate, the value of any specific gifts of those assets is taken to be their reduced value.

The value of any specific gifts on which the relief is *not* available shall be taken to be the appropriate fraction of their value (s 39(A)(3)).

Section 39(A)(4) provides that the appropriate fraction means a fraction of which

(a) the numerator is the difference between the value transferred and the reduced value of the specific gift of relieved property; and

(b) the denominator is the difference between the unreduced value transferred and the unreduced value of the specific gift of relieved property.

It would no doubt assist to reduce this fraction to a formula:

$$\frac{VT - RVG}{UVT - UVG}$$

where:

VT = the value transferred in the estate after deduction of the relief
RVG = the reduced value of any specific gifts of relieved property
UVT = the unreduced value transferred i.e. the value of the estate before relief is deducted and
UVG = the unreduced value of any specific gifts of relieved property

The application of this formula can be illustrated with an example.

EXAMPLE
The testator has a farm valued at £500,000 attracting 50% relief, a florist business valued at £100,000, also attracting 50% relief, and other assets in his estate of £100,000, making a total estate of £700,000.

Under his will he leaves his business to his daughter, subject to any tax thereon, a £200,000 legacy to his widow and the residue to his son.

Under the rules applying before 18 March 1986

Adopting the Inland Revenue practice of attributing the reduced value to specific gifts, the tax would be calculated as follows:

		£
Total estate		700,000
Less relief		300,000
Value transferred		400,000
Legacy to widow	200,000	
Gift to daughter	50,000	250,000
Residue attributable to the son		150,000

Tax would be paid on £200,000 in respect of the gift to the daughter of £50,000 and the residue to the son of £150,000.

Under the new rules

The reduced value of the specific gift to the daughter is £50,000. The appropriate fraction of the value of the gift to the widow is calculated in accordance with the new formula, ie

$$\frac{400,000 \text{ (VT)} - 50,000 \text{ (RVG)}}{600,000 \text{ (UVT)} - 100,000 \text{ (UVG)}} = \frac{350,000}{500,000} = \frac{7}{10}$$

The gift to the widow is therefore multiplied by the appropriate fraction, ie 200,000 × 0.7 = £140,000.

The tax would therefore now be calculated as follows:

		£
Total estate		700,000
Less relief		300,000
Value transferred		400,000
Value attributable to widow's legacy	140,000	
Value attributable to daughter's gift	50,000	190,000
Attributable to the residue to the son		210,000

Tax would now be paid on £260,000, being the gift to the daughter of £50,000 and the gift to the son of £210,000.

For the sake of simplicity (!) it has been assumed that the specific gift to the daughter bears its own tax to avoid the grossing-up provisions in s 38(3)–(5) (see para **10.30**).

Specific gifts of relieved property encouraged

7.74 The overall effect of the new provisions will be to operate in favour of specific gifts of property attracting business and agricultural relief to non-exempt beneficiaries.

RELIEF FOR WOODLANDS (ss 125–130)

7.75 In the case of the previous two reliefs, relief is given in the form of reducing the value of the asset. In the case of woodlands, the relief is given by leaving the value of the property out of account when it is transferred and deferring the charge to tax until there is an ultimate disposal.

7.76 The relief applies in respect of growing trees and underwood, subject to certain conditions, if the value transferred is on a death and an election is made to defer the payment of tax.

Relief only applies on death

7.77 As the relief only applies on death it will not apply to potentially exempt transfers or any other form of lifetime transfer.

Conditions for relief (s 125)

7.78 The relief only applies to trees and underwood growing on land in the UK, but the land itself does not qualify. To qualify for the relief the deceased must either have been beneficially entitled to the property throughout the five years immediately preceding his death or must have become beneficially entitled to it otherwise than for consideration in money or moneys worth, ie by a lifetime gift or on death.

Claim for relief within two years

7.79 A claim for relief must be made by the person liable for the tax who must make an election by notice in writing within two years of the date of death (unless extended by the Board).

Illustration of operation of the relief

7.80 The application of these reliefs can be illustrated as follows:

EXAMPLE

A father dies in 1986 with qualifying timber worth £50,000 and the land on which it is growing worth £10,000, which he leaves to his son subject to tax. The residue of his estate worth £85,000 he leaves to his daughter.

If the son does not elect to defer the payment of the tax, the tax payable on the whole estate will be £25,500, of which £10,552 is borne by the son (50,000 ÷ 145,000 × 25,500) and the balance of £14,948 by the daughter.

If the son elects not to pay the tax, the tax on the estate of £95,000 (the residue plus the land) amounts to £7,200 of which the son pays £758 on the land.

If the son should a year later make a lifetime gift or sell the woodlands, then he would have to pay the marginal rate of tax on the disposition of the timber based on its value at that time. In the present illustration, if there has been no change in the probate value, the son would have to pay tax of £18,300 (the tax between £95,000 and £145,000).

7.81 Using the same illustration, if the son had been killed a year after his father's death with the woodland in his estate, it would be aggregated with the son's estate. If the woodland was virtually the only asset of the son's estate, no tax would be payable as it would fall within the nil band.

7.82 In the light of these provisions, the beneficiary liable to pay the tax must take particular care to consider whether it is advisable to make an election for this relief, particularly in cases where the woodlands are mature.

Property left out of account (s 125)

7.83 If on a death an election is made to defer the payment of the tax, the property is left out of account and therefore no tax is payable in respect of the woodlands on that death. Tax does, however, become payable when the woodlands are subsequently sold or otherwise disposed of (other than on death). Tax is paid on the value of the woodlands at that time less certain qualifying expenses of disposal, replanting and replacement of trees.

Subsequent sale (s 127(1)(a)

7.84 Where the disposal is a sale for full consideration of money or money's worth, tax is levied on the net proceeds of sale less allowable expenses of disposal and replanting in so far as they are not allowable for income tax (s 130).

Subsequent lifetime gift (s 127(1)(b)

7.85 If the disposal is otherwise than by way of sale for full consideration of money or money's worth, the same principle applies with two modifications. First, instead of the net proceeds of sale, an amount equal to the net value of the woodlands at the time of the disposal, less allowable expenses, is substituted. Secondly, if the disposal itself is a chargeable transfer, the value of the transfer is reduced by the amount of tax which now falls due on the disposal by reference to the previous death.

Successive deaths

7.86 Provided there is not a lifetime disposal of the timber, the payment of tax can be postponed indefinitely if it passes on death. When it is ultimately disposed of, the net proceeds are aggregated with the assets of the estate through which it last passed to ascertain the amount of tax. There is no retrospective increase in the amount of tax payable in respect of the other assets in the estate, which therefore means that the whole burden of the marginal rate of tax falls on the net proceeds.

Pass through small estate

7.87 It will therefore be appreciated that the maximum benefit of this relief is achieved if tax (if any) is paid on the woodlands when it passes through a small estate.

Deed of variation to maximise benefit

7.88 If the timber is comprised in a substantial estate and the beneficiary of the timber is himself likely to have a substantial estate, one should consider the possibility of entering into a deed of variation within two years of the death to ensure that the woodlands, particularly if they are becoming mature, pass into the estate of someone who has a lower rate of tax. Indeed, it could be left to the estate of someone who has a small estate and has died within two years of the first death.

Interaction with other reliefs

7.89 If the land qualifies for agricultural property relief, such as if the woodlands are occupied with agricultural land which is ancillary to that of the agricultural land, woodlands relief cannot be claimed.

7.90 If the woodlands are commercially managed then business property relief may be applicable. This does not prevent the persons liable to tax electing for the timber relief and if they do so the value of the timber is left out of account and the business relief is applied to the balance of the property. If an election is not made then the reduction applies to the timber as well.

DOUBLE TAXATION RELIEF

7.91 As inheritance tax is based on an extended meaning of domicile of the transferor (see para **1.18**), on some occasions, particularly on death, there will also be a charge to tax under a foreign jurisdiction. Double taxation may be eliminated or reduced by virtue of a treaty, as provided for in s 158, or by virtue of unilateral relief which may be given in those cases of potential double taxation which are not covered by a treaty (s 159). A detailed consideration of double taxation relief is outside the scope of this Guide.

CHAPTER 8
Settlements

Introduction

8.01 Trusts, rather like companies, have been used for tax avoidance resulting in somewhat complex legislation to prevent abuse. Unfortunately, such legislation also affects trusts established for a genuine purpose. Even in the Middle Ages the device of the 'use' was a method of avoiding feudal dues, which was crudely prevented by 'converting the use' and so destroying a useful early form of trust. In the same way, in modern times there is often the genuine need to set up a trust, but which is sometimes thwarted because of the tax implications. This particularly applied to discretionary trusts after the introduction of capital transfer tax, although the harshness has now been modified to broadly equate the tax on such trusts to that which would have been charged if the funds had not been settled.

8.02 The purpose of this chapter is to consider the definition of the various categories of trusts and the general principles applying to the charge of inheritance tax on such trusts. It is beyond the scope of this Guide to consider the fine detail of such trusts or investigate at length the tax planning aspects, for which reference should be made to Ray *Practical Inheritance Tax Planning* (to be published by Butterworths in 1987) and Courtney *Trust Taxation Manual*. However, the conditions for establishing a maintenance and accumulation trust and trusts for the disabled have been considered in greater detail in view of the special significance they have now been afforded by the FA 1986, whereby creations of or transfers into such favoured trusts are treated as potentially exempt transfers.

8.03 Broadly, where there is a change of an interest in possession in a trust fund, for inheritance tax purposes it is treated as a transfer of value of the underlying assets of the trust fund in which the interest subsists. If there is no change in possession, such as if the settlor settles property on himself for life, no charge to tax will arise at that stage and if the interest in the trust fund passes to an exempt transferee, such as the spouse, the normal exemption will apply.

8.04 Such interest in possession in trusts are usually relatively uncomplicated from a tax point of view, as it is also relatively simple to see if there has been a change of an interest in possession. However, greater problems arise where there is no interest in possession, such as under a discretionary trust where payment of income is only made at the discretion of the trustees and therefore there is no person entitled as of right to the income or to possession of the trust assets. In view of the special rules applying in these situations, these have been dealt with separately at para **8.13** below.

INTEREST IN POSSESSION SETTLEMENTS (ss 49–57)

Beneficial enjoyment equates ownership (ss 49, 50)

8.05 A person beneficially entitled to an interest in possession in settled property is treated as being entitled to the property in which his interest subsists. If he is entitled to part only of the income of the property, then he will be treated as being beneficially entitled to the proportionate part. If a person is entitled to a fixed amount of income from property, then he will be deemed to be beneficially entitled in the proportion which that fixed amount bears to the whole income of the settled property (subject to certain anti-avoidance provisions to prevent the proportion being artificially reduced).

Disposal of beneficial interest (s 51)

8.06 Where a person beneficially entitled to an interest in possession in settled property disposes of it, while such disposition is not itself a transfer of value, tax is charged as if at that time he had made a transfer of value equal to the value of the property in which his interest subsists. If consideration is paid in money or money's worth for that interest, the value in which the interest subsists is reduced by the amount of the consideration given, provided that consideration is extental to that settlement.

Charge on the underlying trust funds (s 52)

8.07 There will therefore be a charge to tax on the underlying trust funds passing on a change of interest in possession, whether this is during a lifetime or on death. The value chargeable will be the value of the underlying trust's assets, contrary to the normal rule that a transfer of value is calculated by reference to the loss to the transferor's estate rather than the benefit to the transferee's estate.

Exemptions

Where no change in beneficial enjoyment (s 53)

8.08 On the principle that there is only a charge where there is a change of interest in possession, there will be no charge to tax where the person who has an interest in possession becomes immediately absolutely entitled to the settled property or to another interest in the property in which his interest subsists. This would apply, for example, where a remainderman surrenders his interest to the life tenant so that the life tenant becomes the absolute owner of the settled property. Further, where settled funds are partitioned between a life tenant and remainderman, the proportion of the fund taken by the life tenant is also exempt and only the property taken by the remainderman is chargeable.

Reverter to settlor (s 54)

8.09 If there is a reversion to the settlor during his lifetime, there is no charge to tax on the termination of that interest in possession when it reverts to the settlor in his lifetime. This exemption, however, does not apply if the settlor acquired a reversionary interest in a property for money or money's worth. Therefore, if a settlor settles property on A for life with reversion back to himself, in the event of A's death during the settlor's lifetime, even though there has been a change of interest in possession back to the settlor, there is no charge to tax.

Reverter to settlor's spouse (s 54)

8.10 A similar exemption applies where there is a 'reversion' to the settlor's spouse either in his lifetime or within two years of his death provided the spouse is domiciled in the UK.

Reversionary interests (ss 55 and 56)

8.11 Where a person entitled to an interest (whether in possession or not) in any settled property acquires a reversionary interest expectant (whether immediately or not) on that interest, the reversionary interest does not form part of his estate (unless the reversionary interest was acquired for a consideration in money or money's worth after 15 April 1976 but before 12 April 1978).

Exempt transferees (s 57)

8.12 Where on the termination of an interest in possession it passes to an exempt transferee, such as to a spouse or to a charity, then the usual exemptions applying to exempt transferees applies. So if property has been settled on A for life with remainder over to his spouse either for life or absolutely, the change in possession is between exempt transferees and therefore no charge to tax arises.

SETTLEMENTS WITHOUT INTERESTS IN POSSESSION (s 58–85)

No person entitled to an interest in possession

8.13 Where under a settlement there is no person entitled to an interest in possession, under the normal rules outlined above, as there is no change of interest in possession in the settled fund during that time, there would be no charge to tax during such time as no person was entitled to an interest in possession.

8.14 Such settlements would arise where the income is to be accumulated, so that no person is entitled to it, or where there is a discretionary settlement whereby the income was paid to beneficiaries not as of right but only at the discretion of the trustees which again would have the result that no person would be entitled to the income or possession of the trust fund.

8.15 At one time, this device of discretionary settlement was an effective method of avoiding estate duty where on death there was no change of interest in possession except on the death of the last discretionary beneficiary. However, as long as there were at least two discretionary beneficiaries, there was no person entitled as of right to the income or possession of the trust fund; therefore no charge to tax would arise on the death of one of several discretionary beneficiaries.

Revision of rules in 1982

8.16 The rules relating to settlements without interests in possession were completely overhauled by the FA 1982 and are now contained in Chapter III of Pt III of the 1984 Act. These new rules endeavour to simplify the earlier provisions and more nearly equate the tax payable on settled property with that which would be broadly comparable for property held absolutely. Under a traditional interest in possession settlement, tax would be payable each time the trust fund passed from one generation to another; under the new provisions, if such a trust continues for $33\frac{1}{3}$ years, effectively tax is paid once on the whole trust fund.

Treatment of favoured trusts

8.17 Certain forms of trusts where there is no interest in possession receive special, favoured, treatment whereby once the tax has been paid on the creation of the trust, they escape the periodic charge and also a charge when the trusts are transferred to an interest in possession. The most important of these are accumulation and maintenance settlements and trusts for the disabled; these trusts now have special significance as creations of or transfers into such favoured trust are treated as potentially exempt transfers whereas the creation of or transfers into other forms of trust are treated as lifetime chargeable transfers.

Creation of the settlement

8.18 The creation of a settlement without interests in possession is treated like any other lifetime chargeable transfer but, unless as mentioned above it is a favoured trust, it will be a lifetime chargeable transfer and not a potentially exempt transfer and therefore be taxed at half the prescribed rate of tax at that stage in its creation or when further funds are paid into the settlement.

Taxation during the subsistence of the trust (the principal charge under s 64)

The ten-year charge

8.19 By virtue of s 64, a charge is imposed on all relevant property comprised in the settlement immediately before a ten-year anniversary.

Relevant property

8.20 Relevant property means property comprised in the settlement in which no interest in possession exists other than principally in accumulation and maintenance settlements, trusts for disabled persons, certain miscellaneous other favoured trusts and excluded property.

The ten-year anniversary

8.21 The ten-year anniversary is defined by s 61(1) as the tenth anniversary of the date on which the settlement commenced (with certain modification for pre-1 April 1983 settlements) and all subsequent anniversaries at ten-yearly intervals.

The rate of charge

8.22 Relevant property held in the trust throughout the ten years before the ten-year anniversary will be charged at 30% of the rate of tax which would have been charged if the funds in the settlement had been settled immediately before the tenth anniversary. In other words, tax is paid at 30% of the lifetime rate which would have been charged if the settlement had been created with the value of the funds comprised in the settlement at the date of the ten-year anniversary.

The property charged

8.23 The value transferred has to be adjusted to include the settled property in which there is no interest in possession (except for excluded property comprised in charitable trusts, accumulation and maintenance settlements, qualifying trusts for the disabled and certain other miscellaneous favoured trusts and excluded property) and the value of any other funds which were settled by the same instrument, together with any funds added after the trust's commencement. There also has to be added the value of any related settlements; two settlements are related if and only if the settlor is the same in each case, and they commenced on the same day.

Pro rata reductions

8.24 Where all the property has not been comprised in the settlement throughout the preceding ten years, there will be a pro rata reduction of one-fortieth for each complete successive quarter in the ten-year period during which the property was not relevant property.

Charges at other times (the interim charge under s 65)

The interim charge

8.25 When the settled property ceases to be relevant property, an 'interim charge' to tax becomes payable, whether the property leaves the settlement when a person becomes absolutely entitled in possession, or stays within the settlement but no longer remains relevant property (such as if it is converted into an accumulation and maintenance or interest in possession trust).

Anti-avoidance provision

8.26 There is an anti-avoidance provision to deter trustees making a disposition (which includes associated operations) reducing the value of the relevant property comprised in the settlement. The trustees must establish that they did not intend to confer any gratuitous benefit on any person and that the transaction was either made at arm's length between unconnected persons, or it was made between connected persons and that it was such that it might be expected to be made in an arm's length transaction between unconnected persons.

Pro rata charge before ten years

8.27 When an interim charge becomes payable before the first ten-year anniversary, it will be calculated pro rata to the length of time it has been in the trust in accordance with the detailed provisions set out in s 68 and based on complete successive quarters in the period beginning with the date on which the settlement commenced.

The rate of charge between anniversaries

8.28 The rate of the interim charge between the ten-year anniversaries is relatively easy to ascertain under s 69. Tax is charged at the rate at which it was charged on the last ten-year anniversary according to the number of complete successive quarters between the last ten-year anniversary and the day before the chargeable event. It is therefore charged in units of one-fortieth.

ACCUMULATION AND MAINTENANCE TRUSTS (s 71)

8.29 Where income from a trust fund is to be accumulated, either by operation of law (such as during a minority under the TA 1925, s 31), or where there is a direction for accumulation, such as 'to my son on attaining 25 and pending attainment of that age the intermediate income shall be accumulated and added to the gift', during such time as the income is to be accumulated, there is no person entitled to an interest in possession. Normally, under the above provisions, there would be a charge to tax on creation of the settlement, a ten-yearly charge during such time as the income is accumulated and also an interim charge when the interest falls into possession.

8.30 However, a certain type of family settlement, an accumulation and maintenance trust which would otherwise fall foul of these provisions, is given privileged treatment provided certain conditions are satisfied.

Conditions to establish trust

8.31 The conditions to be satisfied are contained in s 71. They are that:

(a) one or more persons will, on or before attaining a specified age not exceeding 25, become beneficially entitled to, or to an interest in possession in, the settled property or part of it; and

(b) no interest in possession subsists in the settled property and the income from it is to be accumulated in so far as it is not applied for the maintenance, education or benefit of the beneficiary; and

(c) either:

    (i) not more than 25 years have elapsed since the commencement of the settlement or, if later, since the time when the settled property began to satisfy condition (a) and (b) above; *or*

    (ii) all the persons who are or have been beneficiaries are or were either grandchildren of a common parent, or children, widows or widowers of such grandchildren who were themselves beneficiaries but died before becoming entitled to, or to an interest in possession in, the settled property as mentioned in condition (a) above.

Condition (a)

Interest in possession by the age of 25

8.32 This condition requires that one or more persons will, on or before attaining a specified age not exceeding 25, become entitled to an interest in possession in the settled property. This condition therefore prevents the cumulation period being extended beyond 25 years and requires the beneficiary to take an interest in possession by that age at the latest.

The effect of the TA 1925, s 31

8.33 By virtue of TA 1925, s 31, where there is a gift contingent on the attainment of an age greater than 18, until the attainment of that age, the income is accumulated (in so far as it is not applied at the discretion of the trustees for the maintenance, education or benefit of the beneficiary) but, in the absence of any contrary provision in the trust instrument, on the attainment of majority the beneficiary becomes entitled to the income even though his entitlement to the capital may be postponed.

Condition only requires entitlement to income

8.34 Accordingly, the first condition will be satisfied if by virtue of the TA 1925, s 31, the beneficiary becomes entitled to the income, even though the entitlement to the capital may be postponed to an age exceeding 25.

Accumulation beyond the age of 25

8.35   The difficulty arises, however, if the TA 1925, s 31 is ousted by a provision in the trust instrument that the income is to be accumulated until a beneficiary becomes entitled to the capital. If in these circumstances the age specified exceeds 25, this will not satisfy the first condition. However, if no age is actually specified in the trust deed as to when the beneficiary becomes entitled to the settled property or to an interest in possession in it, by concession relief will be given to these cases if it is otherwise clear from the terms of the trust instrument and the known ages of the beneficiaries, that one or more beneficiaries will become entitled to the settled property, or to an interest in possession in it, by the age of 25, even though such age is not actually specified in the trust instrument.

Contingencies other than attaining 25

8.36   While this condition requires the income to be accumulated for a beneficiary contingently on his attaining a specified age as opposed to any other contingency, the condition will not be breached if there are several contingencies so long as one of them must be satisfied on or before the attainment of a specified age not exceeding 25, such as for example, to a beneficiary contingent on his passing Bar finals or attaining the age of 25, whichever shall first occur.

Condition (b)

No interest in possession subsists and income accumulated

8.37   The second requirement is that no interest in possession subsists in the settled property and that the income from it is to be accumulated so far as it is not applied for the maintenance, education or benefit of the beneficiary contingently entitled on attaining the specified age. The power to apply the income to anyone other than such a beneficiary contingently entitled would take it outside s 71. Further, it is provided that the income *is* to be accumulated, which means that a mere power to accumulate would not be sufficient. It is further required that the only income that can be used is for the maintenance, education or benefit of the beneficiary.

The interest before attaining 25

8.38   When the accumulation period expires on a person becoming entitled to an interest in possession, such as at 18 under the TA 1925, s 31, then no problem arises, as he then becomes entitled to an interest in possession and when he becomes entitled to the capital of the trust fund, such as at the attainment of the age of 25, there is no charge to tax as there is no change of possession. However, a difficulty can arise if after the expiration of the accumulation period no person becomes entitled to the income but discretionary payments are made. The second condition then ceases to be satisfied and the discretionary trusts continue. For example, if property is settled on two one-year old twins and the income is to be accumulated for twenty-one years, in so far as not applied for their maintenance, education or benefit, and the income thereafter is to be distributed between the two beneficiaries at the discretion of the trustees until attainment of the age of 25 years, when the capital is distributed between the two beneficiaries, a charge will then arise.

Condition (c)

Restricted to one generation

8.39 This condition was not originally inserted in the FA 1975, but introduced by the FA 1976, s 106 when it was realised that the relief given to these trusts could be carried over from one generation to the next under settlements containing a power to substitute successive generations for the existing generation of beneficiaries. This condition was therefore inserted to prevent relief being rolled over from one generation to another and it must be satisfied in the case of all settlements made after 15 April 1976.

Postponement limited to 25

8.40 The first alternative of this condition is that not more than 25 years must have elapsed since it become an accumulation and maintenance trust before the beneficiaries thereunder become entitled to an interest in possession. If beneficiaries become entitled to an interest in possession outside the 25-year period then this will fall outside the relief given. This could arise, for example, if property is simply settled on A's children on attaining the age of 25. If there is a direction to accumulate until the age of 25, then if A should subsequently have children they cannot take an interest in possession within the 25 years from the creation of the trust. If there is no direction to accumulate so that the children become entitled to the income at 18, then any children born more than seven years from the commencement of the trust will fall outside these provisions. To avoid such a problem, a power should be inserted enabling the trustees to exclude the TA 1925, so that interests in possession of minors may be accelerated to ensure they become entitled to an interest in·possession during the critical 25-year period.

The common grandparent

8.41 The second alternative extends the relief to the genuine family trust for a period which may exceed 25 years from the date of the original settlement.

The relief given

8.42 Provided all conditions are satisfied, no tax arises when a beneficiary becomes entitled to or to an interest in possession in the settled property. Nor does tax arise on the death of a beneficiary during the accumulation period. However, there is the danger that if the beneficiary becomes entitled by virtue of the TA 1925, s 31 to the income at 18, but payment of the capital is postponed until the age of 25 (or any later period), then the beneficiary will have an interest in possession and the usual charge to tax will arise if he dies before attaining 25.

8.43 The objective of these provisions is therefore to as nearly as possible equate the tax position as if the settlor had gifted the property to the beneficiaries on their attainment of the specified age.

PROTECTIVE TRUSTS (s 88)

Definition

8.44 Settled property is held on protective trusts if 'held on trusts to the like effect as those specified in s 33(1) of the TA 1925'. Broadly, these are two stage trusts for the benefit of 'the principal beneficiary' for the period of his life or any lesser period, under which during that period the income is held on trust for the principal beneficiary until the occurrence of one of the specified events, such as alienation or bankruptcy. On such event, for the rest of the life of the principal beneficiary. the income is held upon discretionary trusts for the benefit of the principal beneficiary, his spouse and issue, if any, or if there is no spouse or issue, for the benefit of the principal beneficiary and 'the persons who would, if he were actually dead, be entitled to the trust property or the income thereof'.

The principal beneficiary treated as life tenant throughout trust

8.45 But for the special treatment afforded to settled property held on protective trusts, on the determination of the principal beneficiary's interest, there would be a charge to tax; but s 88 provides that it is disregarded and the principal beneficiary is effectively treated as being beneficially entitled to an interest in possession of the property during such time as it has been held on protective trusts and no charge arises until the death of the principal beneficiary or the earlier termination of the discretionary trust. Effectively therefore for tax purposes he is treated as having been in possession of the trust throughout.

8.46 If the failure or determination of the principal beneficiary's interest occurred before 11 April 1978, different rules applied, which have now been consolidated in s 73.

TRUSTS FOR DISABLED PERSONS (s 89)

The provisions prior to 10 March 1941

8.47 In respect of property settled before 10 March 1971, s 74 preserves the old rules which basically provide that during the life of a disabled person, where there was no person entitled to an interest in possession, the trust was treated broadly as an interest in possession trust for the life of the disabled person.

The rules after 9 March 1981

8.48 The FA 1981 completely redrew the provisions relating to disabled trusts, and the rules in respect of property settled after 9 March 1981 are now contained in s 89, which broadly adopts the approach of the rules applying to protected trusts. It is provided that where the property is settled after 9 March 1981 and is held on trusts:

(a) under which, during the life of a disabled person, no interest in possession in settled property subsists; and

(b) which secure that no less than half of the settled property which is applied during his life is applied for his benefit,

such person shall be treated as beneficially entitled to an interest in possession in the settled property.

Definition of a disabled person

8.49 A disabled person is defined by s 89(4) as a person who when the property was transferred in settlement:

(a) was incapable, by reason of mental disorder within the meaning of the Mental Health Act 1983, of administering his property or managing his affairs; or

(b) was in receipt of an attendance allowance under s 35 of the

Social Security Act 1975 or the Social Security (Northern Ireland) Act 1975.

The power of advancement to disabled person

8.50 The power of advancement conferred on trustees by the TA 1925, s 32 or the TA (Northern Ireland) 1958, s 33 would not disqualify the trust from favourable treatment. If there is an extended power of advancement as normally incorporated in trust deeds, and if this can be exercised in favour of persons other than a disabled beneficiary, it will take it outside these provisions.

The disabled person is treated as having an interest in possession

8.51 The disabled beneficiary is deemed to have an interest in possession so that if he settles the property on himself, there is no transfer of value.

Accumulation permitted

8.52 Accumulation for such period as the law allows is permitted, which means it is not necessary to pay any income at all to the disabled person or in the case of a mentally disturbed person, to his receiver. However only if income is paid out need at least half of it be applied to the disabled person. This may be of particular relevance if the income of a disabled person from the trust fund would disqualify him from obtaining other social security benefits.

OTHER MISCELLANEOUS FAVOURED TRUSTS

8.53 There are a number of miscellaneous trusts under Chapter IV of Pt III of the 1984 Act which also receive favourable treatment:

(a) trusts for the benefit of employees (s 86), which extends to newspaper trusts (s 87);

(b) a superannuation scheme or fund approved (under s 151) by the Inland Revenue, unless the benefit under the fund or scheme becomes comprised in a discretionary trust, when the person entitled to the benefit is treated as a settlor (s 151(5));

(c) trade or professional compensation funds, where the only or main objects are compensation for or relief of losses or hardship etc (s 58(3)).

CHAPTER 9

Calculation and payment of tax

9.01 The amount of inheritance tax payable is determined by the three principles of cumulation, aggregation and progression.

CUMULATION (s 7)

Seven-year cumulation period

9.02 Inheritance tax is a seven-year cumulative tax (s 7(1) as substituted by the FA 1986, Sch 19, para 2(1)(b)). The principle of cumulation therefore requires that the tax on the present transfer must take account of chargeable transfers already made by the transferor; equally, subsequent transfers within seven years of the present transfer will take account of the present transfer. Finally, on death, all chargeable transfers made within seven years of the date of death are cumulated with the transferor's estate and any other assets charged at that time (see para **4.04**).

Reportable transfers

9.03 Therefore, on death, it will be necessary to ascertain all chargeable transfers made in the period of seven years before the date of his death even if returns have not been made of those transfers. At present no return needs to be made where the total of a person's transfer in any tax year does not exceed £10,000 and where his cumulative total transfers in the last seven years does not exceed £40,000. This will therefore now only apply to lifetime chargeable transfers, as potentially exempt transfers do not become chargeable transfers unless and until the transferor fails to survive seven years. The importance of reporting transfers in time is illustrated at para **4.04**(8).

Settled funds passing

9.04 It is therefore the total of the gross cumulative chargeable transfers made within seven years of the present transfer which must be cumulated for ascertaining the tax payable on the present transfer.

Transfers which are of settled property, such as when a beneficial interest in possession terminates, must also be cumulated. So if property is settled on A for life with remainder to B and A surrenders his life interest to B, there would be a chargeable transfer of value equal to the value of the settled property at that time.

The value to be cumulated

9.05 The values to be cumulated are those transferred by chargeable transfers. Therefore if the relief takes the form of a reduction in the value of the property and therefore in the value transferred, such as business property relief or agricultural property relief, it is the reduced value which is cumulated. If the relief takes the form of a reduction by credit of tax such as quick succession relief (see para **4.28**) or the tapered relief within seven years of death for lifetime chargeable transfers and potentially exempt transfers (see paras **2.15** and **3.05** respectively) or double taxation relief (see para **7.91**) the whole value transferred must be cumulated.

9.06 This can be illustrated with an example.

EXAMPLE
A, who has made no previous chargeable transfers, makes a chargeable transfer of £77,000 to a close company in July 1986. The tax chargeable will be nil, because utilising the previous and current years' annual exemptions the transfer is within the nil band. However, A's cumulative total is therefore now £71,000. If in the following month A transfers a further £14,000 to the same company, if the tax is borne by the company, this will amount to £3,600 and A's cumulative total will now be £95,000. Therefore should he make any further chargeable transfers or die within seven years of the first transfer, then the tax thereon would be paid at the rates appropriate from £95,000 upwards. If, however, the tax is borne by A, the gift must be grossed up as detailed at para **3.13**.

Death within seven years of the transfer

9.07 Before the FA 1986 the priciple of cumulation was relatively simple. Whether a particular transfer of value was chargeable was generally known at the time of making the transfer and although the subsequent death of the transferor within three years of the transfer would increase the tax payable on chargeable transfers made in that time, it still did not affect the cumulative total of chargeable transfers.

9.08 Before 18 March 1986 reassessment of the cumulative totals would normally only be necessary in the event of the now abolished exemption of mutual transfers applying (see para **5.35**) or in the event of a voidable transfer being avoided (see para **5.34**).

Reassessments

9.09 However, in respect of transfers made after 17 March 1986, quite apart from the reassessment of any tax payable, reassessments of the cumulative totals will be necessary in a number of circumstances in the event of the transferor dying within seven years of the transfer. These reassessments will arise in the following cases:

(1) *Potentially exempt transfers*, ie if these become chargeable transfers by virtue of the death of the transferor within seven years of the date of the transfers (see para **2.11**);

(2) *Property subject to a reservation*. If a gift of property subject to a reservation ceases to be so subject within seven years before the date of death, it is converted into a potentially exempt transfer (see para **2.27**) and immediately therefore into a chargeable transfer. However, if the gift remains subject to a reservation up to the date of death, this does not affect the cumulative lifetime totals but, of course, will be aggregated with the estate (see para **2.28**).

(3) *Loss of business property or agricultural property relief*, ie if either of these reliefs is lost by virtue of the transferee making a lifetime disposition within seven years of the date of death of the transferor, as this will increase the value transferred by such transfers (see paras **7.12** and **7.59** respectively);

(4) *Voidable transfers*. In the event of a voidable transfer being declared void it is treated as though it had never been made (see para **5.34**).

AGGREGATION

Assets charged on the same event

9.10 Where more than one asset or fund is chargeable on the same event, then all the chargeable assets or funds are aggregated or added together for ascertaining the rate and amount of tax payable and then the total tax so calculated is apportioned for payment between the respective assets or funds pro rata to the value thereof.

9.11 The occasion on which this principle most frequently operates is death, when all assets chargeable on the death are aggregated together, as illustrated in para **4.10**.

9.12 The principle, however, may also be relevant to lifetime transfers. This may arise if a person settles say land, shares and cash together. The tax is shared rateably between the different assets pro rata to their value unless, of course, the tax is borne by the settlor when in addition the gift will have to be grossed up.

9.13 Where different funds pass in different directions, the amount of tax borne by each fund is increased. So if a deceased has a free estate of £50,000 and a life interest in a settled fund valued at £100,000, the total tax is based on £150,000, which will then be rateably apportioned between the estate and the settled fund so that the free estate will bear a one-third share and the settled fund two-thirds of the total tax.

Transfers made in one day (s 266)

Apportioned rateably

9.14 Where two or more transfers are made on the same day, they are added together and treated as a single transfer and the tax then apportioned pro rata to the respective transfers. So if a settlor, who has already utilised his annual exemptions, creates two interests in possession trusts on the same day with £40,000 in one settlement and £60,000 in the other settlement, the total tax, assuming that the trusts bear their own tax, will be £4,475, 40% of which will be apportioned to the first trust and 60% of which will be apportioned to the second trust.

Order most favourable to taxpayer

9.15 Where a person makes more than one chargeable transfer on the same day, the total value transferred may, because of the grossing-up rule, depend on the order in which the transfers were made. However, it is provided by s 266(1) that when this occurs they should be treated in the order which results in the lowest value chargeable. This would therefore normally be the gift which is grossed up being treated as having been made first so it is grossed up at a lower point on the progressive scale.

9.16 If, of course, it is desired to alter the order of transfers then they should be made on separate days.

PROGRESSION

9.17 The principle of progression is an inherent feature in the scale of tax rates—the greater the value transferred, the higher the rate of tax attracted.

The single tax Table

9.18 Prior to 18 March 1986, there were two Tables, one for tax on lifetime transfers (which after 12 March 1984 has been at half the death rate) and the second which applied to transfers on death or transfers made within three years of death. By the FA 1986, there is now only one Table applying which is equivalent to the previous death Table. However, lifetime chargeable transfers are taxed at exactly half the rate in the single prescribed Table.

The Tables in the Appendices

9.19 Appendix B contains the current single Table entitled 'Death rates'. Below this, for convenience, is also shown a Table entitled 'Half rates' which shows the tax applicable on lifetime chargeable transfers at half the death rates. In both cases the Tables have been extended to include cumulative chargeable transfers (net) for grossing-up purposes. Appendix C contains the death and lifetime rates operating from 6 April 1985 to 17 March 1986 for capital transfer tax. Appendix D contains the rates from 13 March 1984 to 5 April 1985 and Appendix E contains the rates from 15 March 1983 to 12 March 1984. Earlier Tables can be found in *Whillans's Tax Tables*.

Later gifts bear higher tax

9.20 The progressive nature of the tax results in earlier transfers bearing no tax at all or only tax at the lower rates whereas subsequent transfers will be taxed at a progressively higher rate, until on death the estate and any assets aggregated with the estate will bear the full brunt of the marginal rate of tax. This is a factor which a testator should keep in mind when disposing of his free estate.

Use of tax Table

When the transferee pays the tax

9.21 Where the transferee bears the tax, it is simply calculated by ascertaining the total gross chargeable transfers made by the transferor to date. This will determine at what point in the Table the transferee will start to pay tax. The amount of tax is then simply calculated by reference to each of the bands and divided by half (as lifetime transfers) or alternatively, the 'Half rates' Table may be used and the tax calculated directly. So, for example, if the transferor having utilised his annual exemption, makes a gift into a company of £100,000, tax of £3,600 will be payable on the first £95,000 of the transfer and the balance of £5,000, being in the next band, will bear tax at 17½%, viz £875, making total tax payable of £4,475.

Grossing up lifetime gifts where transferor pays the tax

9.22   If the transferor agrees to pay the tax on the transfer, then the loss to his estate is the amount of the gift plus the tax on that tax, etc. Usually this now only applies to lifetime chargeable transfers. The grossing-up principle and calculation is explained at para **3.13**.

Grossing up specific gifts in a will

9.23   As the value attributable to a specific gift corresponds to the value of the gift (s 38(1)), if a gift is paid tax free, the value of the gift to the beneficiary is the grossed-up amount of the gift. In certain circumstances it is therefore necessary to gross up the value of the gift at the death rates. This is explained and illustrated at para **10.33**. The Tables are used in exactly the same way, except it is the 'cumulative chargeable transfers (net)' column of the 'Death rates' Table which is used rather than the 'Half rates' Table.

PAYMENT OF TAX

9.24   In this chapter must finally be considered three more aspects of inheritance tax: the date the tax falls due for payment; the interest payable on the tax; and whether the tax may be paid by instalments.

Date due for payment of tax (s 226)

On death

9.25   On death, tax falls due six months after the end of the month in which the death occurs. This applies to:

(1)   the free estate;
(2)   any additional tax which becomes payable in respect of a lifetime chargeable transfer;
(3)   any tax that becomes payable in respect of a potentially exempt transfer, which becomes a chargeable transfer;

(4)   tax which becomes due on property which is still subject to a reservation at date of death;

(5)   any additional tax which becomes payable in respect of a gift to a political party exceeding £100,000, where the transferor dies within one year of the transfer;

(6)   an interest passing under a settlement on death.

Other transfers

9.26   In all other cases, that is lifetime chargeable transfers and the charge in respect of settled property (other than when it is on a death, as above), payment will fall due depending on the date on which the transfer was made. If made after 5 April and before 1 October in any year, the tax falls due on 30 April of the following year. If the transfer was made after 30 September and before 5 April in any tax year, payment falls due six months from the end of the month in which the transfer was made. Therefore, by careful timing, the payment of the tax can be postponed by over a year; for example, if the transfer was made on 6 April in one year, payment does not fall due until 30 April in the following year.

Payment by instalments (ss 227–229)

Lifetime transfers

9.27   If the transferor pays the tax there is no option to pay by instalments in respect of lifetime transfers (with the exception of woodlands) and he must pay it on the due date and interest will run thereafter. If, however, the transferee pays the tax, provided it is qualifying property as described below, he can by so electing in writing to the Inland Revenue pay the tax by ten equal yearly instalments. This facility to pay the tax by ten yearly instalments applies to chargeable transfers made after 14 March 1983. Before that date different rules applied, whereby payment was made by eight equal yearly instalments or sixteen equal half-yearly instalments; these rules continue to apply in respect of chargeable transfers made before 15 March 1983.

Transfers on death

Personal representatives and beneficiaries of the free estate
9.28   Where the tax arises on death, the personal representatives or other persons (such as trustees or beneficiaries under the will liable to pay the tax) paying the tax on property attracting a charge on death, can elect to pay tax on qualifying property by ten equal yearly

instalments. The election must be made by notice in writing to the Inland Revenue and the first instalment falls due six months after the end of the month in which the death occurred.

Other persons paying the tax
9.29 The option to pay by instalments extends to the tax payable by the other persons in the situations mentioned in para **9.25** above.

Settled property

9.30 The trustees of a settlement and other persons liable for the tax (such as beneficiaries) on settled property attracting a charge can elect to pay tax on qualifying property by ten equal yearly instalments. This extends to charges where there is a termination of an interest in possession, and periodic and other charges in relation to settled property where there is no interest in possession.

Property qualifying for instalment option (ss 227–229)

9.31 The property qualifying for this instalment option is as follows:

(1) Land of any description, wherever situated. This would therefore include leasehold and freehold property and also foreign property. It does not, however, extend to any estate, interest or right by way of mortgage or other security (exemption from definition of land under s 272).

(2) Quoted or unquoted shares or securities of a company which immediately before the chargeable transfer gave control of the company to the deceased, in the case of a transfer on death, to the trustees, in the case of settlements without an interest in possession, and, in any other case, the transferor. A person has 'control' if he has the control of powers of voting on all questions, or on any particular question affecting the company as a whole which, if exercised, would yield the majority of the votes capable of being exercised thereon. For this purpose, a person is attributed the power inherent in shares and securities which are related property (such as held by his spouse) or in which he has an interest in possession (such as life tenant) under a settlement.

(3) Unquoted shares or securities of a company which did not give the transferor control, provided:
    (a) in the case of a chargeable transfer arising on death, at least 20% of the tax payable by the accountable party (liable in the same capacity) is in respect of those shares or

securities or any other shares or securities qualifying for the instalment option under (1)–(4) of para **9.31**; or

(b) the Inland Revenue are satisfied that the tax attributable to the shares and securities cannot be paid in one sum without undue hardship.

(4) Unquoted shares (but not securities) of a company which did not give the transferor control, provided the value of those shares exceeds £20,000 (the figure was £5,000 if the transfer was before 15 March 1983) and either:

(a) the nominal value of the shares is not less than 10% of the nominal value of all the shares of the company at the time of the transfer; or

(b) the shares are ordinary shares and their nominal value is not less than 10% of the nominal value of all ordinary shares of the company at that time.

Ordinary shares are defined as shares which carry either a right to dividends not restricted to dividends at a fixed rate or shares carrying a right to convert into such shares.

(5) A business or an interest in a business (such as sole trader or a partner):

(a) a business includes a profession or vocation, but does not include a business carried on otherwise than for gain;

(b) it is only the net value of the business assets (including goodwill) which qualifies for the instalment option.

Sale or lifetime transfer terminates the option

9.32 If the property qualifying for the instalment option is sold (or pro rata if partial sale), or the transferee makes a chargeable lifetime transfer of the property before the instalments are paid, the balance of the instalments become payable forthwith. This does not extend to transfers which are not chargeable (such as between spouses), nor where the subsequent transfer of the property is on a death. In the case of a settlement, if property ceases to be comprised in the settlement, the outstanding instalments fall due forthwith.

Disposal of potentially exempt transfer precludes the option

9.33 It is specifically provided by s 227(1A) and (1B) (inserted by the FA 1986, Sch 19, para 31(1)) that the option to pay by instalments is lost if the property transferred by a potentially exempt transfer is disposed of by the transferee before the date of death of the transferor or, if earlier, the date of death of the transferee.

Woodlands (s 229)

9.34 Where tax has been deferred from a previous owner's death, the instalment option is available to both the transferor and the transferee if an election is so made, the first instalment being payable six months after the end of the month in which the transfer was made [see para **7.73**]. On woodlands generally, see para **7.75**.

The payment of interest

9.35 Interest runs from the date on which payment of the tax was due. If the chargeable transfer was made on death or is a potentially exempt transfer, the rate is 9%. In any other case the rate is 11% (s 233(2) substituted by the FA 1986, Sch 19, para 32).

Property qualifying for interest free instalments

9.36 Interest is also payable on property which qualifies for the instalment option from the date on which the tax falls due. To this there is the exception that where the instalment option is exercised in respect of property qualifying for business property relief, agricultural property relief or on timber, interest only begins to run on instalments as they fall due.

9.37 This favourable treatment, however, does not apply to two categories of assets on which the instalment option is available namely:

(a) Land, except land which qualifies for agricultural property relief or which is a business asset, otherwise than a business disqualified in para (b) below;

(b) Shares or securities of a company wholly or mainly involved in dealing with securities, stocks or shares, land or buildings or in making or holding investments unless the company is primarily a holding company of qualifying shares or securities, or the business of the company is that of a market maker or discount house in the UK (s 234(3)(c)).

Interest on overpaid tax (s 235)

9.38 If tax has been overpaid, then the excess tax carries interest at the prescribed rate, such interest being tax free.

Pre-10 March 1981 transfers of agricultural property
9.39 Where tax is still being paid by instalments on property qualifying for agricultural property relief in respect of transfers made

before 10 March 1981, these instalments will be by eight annual instalments or sixteen half yearly instalments. Where, however, the tax liability arose before that date, the instalments are not tax free.

CHAPTER 10

Accountability and incidence of tax

Introduction

10.01 The subject of accountability determines who is liable to account to the Crown for inheritance tax: the person or persons to whom the Inland Revenue may look for payment. In many instances there will be more than one person liable to account for the tax. In such circumstances, the liability will be joint and several: the Inland Revenue can claim the whole tax due from any one of them and the person paying will have to recoup it from a third party or out of an asset.

10.02 The subject of incidence determines on whom the ultimate tax burden will fall: how the tax is to be borne between the various beneficiaries.

10.03 When and how the tax due is paid may vary depending by whom it is paid and the nature of the property which is the subject of the tax. This has already been considered in Chapter 9.

ACCOUNTABILITY

10.04 The persons liable to account to the Inland Revenue for the tax arising on a chargeable transfer vary according to the type of disposition. This will normally fall into one of five categories: lifetime chargeable transfers; potentially exempt transfers; gifts with reservation; transfers on death; and transfers of settled property.

Lifetime chargeable transfers (s 199)

Liability for the initial tax

10.05 In the case of a lifetime chargeable transfer of property which is not settled, the persons liable to pay the tax are:

(a)   the transferor;
(b)   the transferee (namely any person the value of whose estate is

increased by the transfer);
(c)   so far as the tax is attributable to the value of any property, any person in whom the property is vested (whether beneficially or otherwise) at any time after the transfer or who at any time is beneficially entitled to an interest in possession in the property (this does not extend to a purchaser unless an Inland Revenue charge has been registered); and
(d)   where by the chargeable transfer any property becomes comprised in a settlement, any person for whose benefit any of the property or income from it is applied.

Primary liability on the transferor

10.06   The primary liability for the tax therefore falls on the transferor and only if it remains unpaid after the date on which it is due to be paid will the Inland Revenue then have recourse to the transferee and the other persons mentioned in the section. Further, if a transferee is called upon to pay the tax in respect of a gift which has been grossed up because the transferor was to pay the tax, to the extent that the transferor has not paid the tax, the value of the gift will be reduced.

Additional liability where transferor dies within seven years

Primary liability on transferee
10.07   The primary liability falls on the transferee in respect of any additional tax payable following the death of the transferor within seven years of the transfer.

Liability on the personal representatives
10.08   If the transferor should die within seven years of the transfer, it is now provided by the substitution of a new sub-cl (2) in s 199 (inserted by the FA 1986, Sch 19, para 26) that any additional tax which becomes payable in the event of the transferor dying within seven years of the transfer shall also be a liability of the transferor's personal representatives. This appears to be reversal of the previous rule under the original sub-s (2), which provided that the liability of the transferor did not extend to any additional tax which may become payable as a result of the transferor dying within three years of the transfer. Liability is, however, limited to the assets mentioned in para **10.15** below. The primary liability in these circumstances, however, remains on the transferee (s 204(8) inserted by the FA 1986, Sch 19, para 28(3)). Nevertheless, if in fact the personal representatives do pay the tax under these new provisions, then it would appear necessary to gross up the gift.

Potentially exempt transfers

Primary liability on transferee

10.09 The primary liability for the payment of the tax in respect of potentially exempt transfers which become chargeable transfers by reason of the death of the transferor within seven years of the transfer, falls on the transferee (s 203(8) inserted by the FA 1986, Sch 19, para 28(3)).

Liability of the personal representatives

10.10 Any tax which becomes payable in respect of potentially exempt transfers shall also be a liability of the transferor's personal representatives (s 199(2), inserted by the FA 1986, Sch 19 para 36). Liability is, however, limited to the assets mentioned in para 10.15 below. If the personal representatives do pay under these circumstances then once again it would appear necessary to gross up the value of the gift.

Gifts with reservation

10.11 Once again the primary liability for the tax on property subject to reservation is on the donee (FA 1986, Sch 19, paras 28(3), 29).

Transfer on death (s 200)

Accountable persons

10.12 The persons liable for the tax on a chargeable transfer on the death of any person are:

(a) the deceased's personal representatives, in so far as the tax is attributable to property which was not immediately before the death comprised in a settlement or if it was settled and consists of land in the UK which devolved upon or vests in the personal representatives;

(b) in so far as the tax is attributable to the value of property which, immediately before the death, was comprised in a settlement, the trustees of the settlement;

(c) in so far as the tax is attributable to the value of any property, any person in whom the property is vested (whether beneficially or otherwise) at any time after the death, or who at such time is beneficially entitled to an interest in possession in the property;

(d) in so far as the tax is attributable to the value of any property which, immediately before the death, was comprised in the settlement, any person for whose benefit any of the property or income from it is applied after the death.

The liability of the personal representatives

10.13   The primary liability is therefore that of the deceased's personal representatives in respect of the free estate or settled land in the UK which actually vests in them, such as where a strict settlement comes to an end on the death of the tenant for life.

10.14   The personal representatives for this purpose include any person or persons who intermeddle in the estate and render themselves executors 'de son tort': *New York Breweries Co v AG* and *IRC v Stype Investments (Jersey) Ltd.*

10.15   The liability of the personal representatives is limited to the extent of assets which they receive as personal representatives, or which they might have so received but for their own neglect or default, which extends to any property received by the personal representatives in settled land (s 204(1), (8), the latter inserted by the FA 1986, Sch 19, para 28(3)).

Liability of the trustees of a settlement

10.16   The trustees of a settlement are liable for tax payable on the death of a beneficiary, such as where there is a settlement and it continues after the death of the life tenant. The liability of the trustees is limited to the amount of property the trustees actually receive or dispose of or become liable to account for to beneficiaries and also such other property which would have been available to the trustees but for their own neglect or default.

Liability of beneficiaries

10.17   Beneficiaries under a will or intestacy and any other person in whom the property vests after the death are also liable, including any transferees from those persons, except for a bona fide purchaser for money or money's worth who will only be bound if the property is subject to an Inland Revenue charge. The liability, however, is limited to the value of property vested in him or in which he enjoys a beneficial interest in possession.

10.18   Further, any beneficiary under a discretionary settlement is liable to the extent of any amount he receives.

Settled property (s 201)

10.19 The persons liable for tax on the value transferred by a chargeable transfer arising on settled property are:

(a) the trustees of the settlement;
(b) any person entitled (whether beneficially or not) to an interest in possession in the settled property;
(c) any person for whose benefit any of the settled property or income from it is applied at or after the time of the transfer;
(d) where the transfer is made during the lifetime of the settlor and the trustees have not for the time being been resident in the UK, the settlor. The settlor, however, shall not be liable to the extent that the tax is increased as a result of him dying within seven years of making the settlement.

Joint tenancies

10.20 The surviving joint tenant or tenants are both trustees and beneficiaries and as such liable to account for the tax payable on the death of a joint tenant whose share passes to them by survivorship.

Political parties (s 206)

10.21 If the transferor has made a gift to a political party exceeding £100,000 and dies within 12 months of that transfer, the amount over that figure is liable to tax; this is the primary liability of the transferee. The excess over £100,000 will, therefore, be a chargeable transfer on the date on which it was made, which will therefore have the effect of increasing the tax on any subsequent lifetime transfers and the marginal rates of tax on the estate.

INCIDENCE

10.22 The persons primarily accountable for tax are normally those persons in whom the asset vests, such as personal representatives, trustees, donees of lifetime gifts in respect of additional tax, etc. While these persons are liable to account for the tax to the Inland Revenue, the distribution of the burden of the tax between the beneficiaries then has to be determined; this is the subject of incidence.

Lifetime gifts

10.23 While both the transferor and transferee are liable to pay the tax, the incidence of the tax is a matter to be determined between themselves. Both are liable to the Inland Revenue and if the transferor fails to account for the tax on the due date, the Inland Revenue will have recourse to the donee. There are certain advantages in the donee paying the tax. It will not be necessary for the gift to be grossed up (although there is no difference in the tax if it is looked at in terms of the donee receiving a net figure). Further, the transferee may in certain situations pay by instalments [see para **9.27**].

Settled property

10.24 Tax would normally (subject to any other directions that may have been given in the trust deed as to the payment of tax) be payable out of the capital of the trust fund, so reducing the fund on which the income is paid to the beneficiaries. The trustees of a settlement may also have recourse to any trust moneys in their hands for the purpose of paying tax attributable to any other property held on the same trusts, but this does not override any direction in the trust deed that the tax should be provided from another source.

A deceased's free estate in the UK (s 211)

10.25 Under estate duty, in the absence of any contrary provision in the will, estate duty in respect of real property was borne by the devisee. The reason for this rule is largely historical. When estate duty was introduced, real property passed direct to the devisee and not to the personal representatives and although subsequently all property comprised in the free estate passed to the personal representatives, the original provision that a devisee bore his own duty was not changed. This rule, however, was subject to any contrary provision in the will and in many cases it was in fact overridden by a provision that all duty should be borne out of the residue.

Re Dougall

10.26 When capital transfer tax was introduced, it was thought that the estate duty provisions continued to apply. However, the decision of the Scottish courts in *Re Dougall* decided that where a will contained no provision to the contrary, tax on all the assets comprised in the free estate were to be borne out of the residue. There was a period of uncertainty as to whether or not this case applied to English estates. The Inland Revenue's attitude was that they would accept any decision agreed between the beneficiaries as to the incidence of the tax, but if no agreement could be reached, then they would adopt the ruling of *Re Dougall*.

Deaths after 25 July 1983

10.27 The matter was finally resolved by the Finance (No 2) Act 1983 s 13(3) (now s 211 of the 1984 Act) in respect of deaths after 25 July 1983. It is now provided that tax on a deceased's free estate situate in the UK and passing to his personal representatives shall be treated as part of the general testamentary administration expenses of the estate in the absence of any contrary provision in the will. This does not extend to foreign assets which bear their own tax.

Review of earlier wills

10.28 Therefore, if any assets are now to bear their own tax, this must be specifically provided in the will. Furthermore, it is important to look at any existing wills made before the 26 July 1983 (or before the draftsman became aware of those provisions!) to ensure that the testator's wishes with regard to incidence will now be effected. However, existing wills which refer to estate duty or capital transfer tax will have effect as if the reference included a reference to inheritance tax chargeable on death.

Summary of incidence

10.29 Obviously the incidence of tax is a vital consideration to any testator and it may be helpful at this stage to summarise the position so that if necessary the testator may in his will make provision for payment of the tax out of his estate which will effectively be treated as a legacy of the amount of tax payable:

(1) *Lifetime chargeable transfers.* Unless these fell within the nil band, tax at half the normal rate would have been paid at the time; but the burden of any increase in the tax by reason of the transferor dying within seven years will be borne by the transferee (see para **10.07**);

(2) *Potentially exempt transfers.* Unless these fall within the nil band, the tax payable will be the liability of the transferee in the event of them becoming chargeable transfers by reason of the death of the transferor within seven years of the transfer (see para **10.09**). Furthermore, this will also necessitate re-assessment of any subsequent transfers as illustrated in para **2.20**, and may also result in a subsequent lifetime chargeable transfer being chargeable for the first time.

(3) *Gifts with reservation.* These gifts will bear their own tax and the liability is that of the donee (see para **10.11**) and furthermore, because they are aggregated with the estate, will bear the marginal rate of tax with the estate (see para **2.28**).

(4) *Trust property*. Tax will normally be borne by the trust assets (see para **10.19**).

(5) *Property passing by survivorship*. This is borne by the survivors (see para **10.20**).

(6) *Foreign property*. This bears its own tax (see para **10.27**).

(7) *The free estate*. As indicated above, the tax on the free estate is borne out of the residue in the absence of any contrary provision (see para **10.27**).

ALLOCATION OF EXEMPTIONS (ss 36–42)

10.30 Chapter III of Pt III of the 1984 Act contains provisions for allocating exemptions on transfers which are not wholly exempt. In practice it is most likely to arise on the distribution of an estate on death where there is a will containing some gifts to chargeable beneficiaries and others to exempt beneficiaries, such as to a spouse or charity.

10.31 No difficulty arises where the whole of the estate is exempt, as simply no tax is payable. Nor is there any difficulty if all the gifts are chargeable. However, because of the rule that a transfer to an exempt transferee cannot be directly taxed on that gift, the provisions to ensure this can sometimes be relatively complex.

Exempt specific gifts

10.32 A specific gift to an exempt transferee must be paid free of tax, regardless of the terms of the will (s 41(a)). An exempt gift of the residue may, however, effectively bear tax as if tax has been paid on specific gifts; this reduces the amount available for distribution.

Exempt share of residue

10.33 However, a gift of a share of the residue which is exempt cannot bear any part of the tax attributable to non-exempt beneficiaries (s 41(b)).

The value attributable to a specific gift

10.34 The value transferred attributable to a specific gift corresponds to the value of the gift (s 38(1)). Therefore, if the gift is paid tax free, the value of the gift is the grossed-up amount of the gift. If it were otherwise, it would be possible to manipulate the exemptions to provide a higher net gift to a chargeable beneficiary than if the gift had been made to that beneficiary outright.

EXAMPLE

A father wishes to give his son his entire estate of £317,000. If he makes a will giving the entire estate to his son, the tax will be £110,500, leaving the son with £206,500. If the father instead gives his son a legacy of £245,000, free of tax, and the residue to charity, and tax was only paid on that net figure of £245,000, which amounts to £71,500, the balance after tax of £500 goes to the charity, saving the son £38,500!

To prevent this, the benefit received by a specific legatee or devisee must be grossed up at the *death rate* to represent the true value of the gift before attributing the balance to the residue under s 39.

10.35 The principle, therefore, is simple, but some of the computations are more complex and can be best illustrated by considering a number of combinations with examples where appropriate. All the following examples assume that there have been no lifetime gifts cumulated with the estate nor any assets which are aggregated with the estate on death, as otherwise, of course, the amount of tax will be increased accordingly.

All gifts to exempt beneficiaries

10.36 Where the whole of the estate is exempt, such as where there is a legacy to a charity and the residue to a spouse, no tax is payable and the estate is distributed accordingly.

All gifts to chargeable beneficiaries

10.37 If all the gifts in the will are chargeable, again there is no great difficulty. The tax is calculated on the entire estate and then apportioned between the beneficiaries whose gifts are subject to tax. There are three possibilities.

Specific gifts all subject to tax

10.38 Tax is calculated on the whole estate and then rateably apportioned between the specific gift and the residue. So if a testator of an estate of £100,000 leaves a legacy of £25,000 subject to tax to his daughter and the residue to his son, the tax on £100,000 of £8,950 is apportioned as to one-quarter to his daughter and three-quarters to his son.

All specific gifts tax free

10.39 Tax is calculated on the whole estate, the specific gifts paid in full and the tax borne by the residue. If in the last example the legacy to the daughter had been free of tax, the legacy would have been paid in full and the tax of £8,950 borne out of the residue.

Some specific gifts tax free and others subject to tax

10.40 In this situation the tax on the whole estate is first calculated and is then apportioned between the taxable specific gifts and the whole of the estate (including the tax free legacies). So if a testator with an estate of £100,000 leaves a legacy of £20,000 tax free to A, a legacy of £30,000 subject to tax to B and the residue of £50,000 to C, the tax on the whole estate of £100,000 will be £8,950, three-tenths of which will be borne by B (£2,685) and the balance borne by the residue (£6,265).

Specific gift exempt, residue chargeable

10.41 If there is a specific gift which is exempt, with the whole of the residue being chargeable, only the amount of the residue will be charged to tax. So, for example, if the total estate is £129,000 and there is a specific legacy to a charity of £34,000, the residue will simply pay tax on £95,000, viz £7,200.

Specific gift chargeable bearing its own tax, residue exempt

10.42 Where there is a specific gift to a chargeable beneficiary and the residue to an exempt beneficiary, again there is little difficulty, as the specific gift will pay the tax on that gift and the residue will pass free of tax. So if a testator with an estate of £129,000 leaves a legacy to his son of £95,000 subject to tax and the residue to charity, the son will receive his legacy less the tax thereon of £7,200, ie £87,800. The charity will receive the balance of £34,000.

Specific gift chargeable freè of tax, residue exempt

10.43 If, however, in the last example the specific gift to the son is given free of tax, the value of the gift to the son will be the amount of the legacy of £95,000, plus the tax attributable to that legacy. This will therefore necessitate a grossing up of the legacy. The legacy grossed up will be £106,077 (£95,000 plus the grossed-up tax of £11,077). The legacy of £95,000 is then simply paid, the tax is paid, which leaves a residue payable to the charity of £22,923.

Exempt specific gift, residue partly exempt

10.44 Where there is an exempt specific gift and the residue has been left partly to an exempt transferee and partly to a chargeable transferee, the specific exempt legacy is disregarded and the share of the residue passing to the non-exempt beneficiary taxed on the amount received.

EXAMPLE

A testator, who has an estate of £240,000, leaves a legacy to his wife of £50,000 and the residue of £190,000 equally between his wife and his daughter. The wife will receive her legacy and her half share of the residue tax free, and the other half of the residue of £95,000 will bear the tax of £7,200 before being paid to the daughter.

Chargeable specific gift subject to tax, partly exempt residue

10.45 Where there is a chargeable specific gift subject to tax, but with a partly exempt, partly taxable, residue, it is simply necessary to calculate the exempt residue by deducting the legacy and dividing the balance between the residuary beneficiaries. The tax on the legacy and non-exempt portion of the estate will then be calculated and apportioned pro rata to their values.

EXAMPLE

A testator leaves a legacy of £50,000 to his son subject to tax and the residue of £200,000 equally between his wife and daughter. The wife must receive her half share of the residue of £100,000 tax free. This leaves the legacy of £50,000 and the other half of the residue of £100,000 to be taxed. The tax on £150,000 is £27,500, one-third of which will be borne by the son and the two-thirds by the daughter.

Chargeable specific gift free of tax, partly exempt residue

10.46 If the total chargeable specific gifts would by themselves attract tax (after cumulating with them chargeable lifetime gifts), the calculation is somewhat more complicated as the value attributable to the specific tax free gifts must first be calculated by reference to an assumed rate on a hypothetical estate in accordance with s 38(5).

EXAMPLE

A testator with an estate of £201,000, gives a tax free legacy to his son of £85,000 and leaves the residue of his estate equally between his wife and daughter.

The following steps are therefore necessary:

(1) Gross up the tax free legacy:
$$£85,000 + £6,000 = £91,000$$
(2) Calculate the residue:
$$£201,000 - £91,000 = £110,000$$

(3)   Arrive at chargeable share:
$$\tfrac{1}{2} \text{ of } £110,000 = £55,000$$
(4)   Total (2) and (3) together to arrive at a hypothetical chargeable estate of £165,000. This is a hypothetical chargeable estate as it is more than the actual estate (£165,000 + widow's £55,000 is £220,000, not £201,000).
(5)   Calculate tax on (4):
$$£33,550$$
(6)   Calculate assumed rate (it is assumed because it is a hypothetical estate):
$$\frac{33,500}{165,000} \times 100 = 20.3\%$$
(7)   Gross up legacy at the assumed rate:
$$£85,000 \times \frac{100}{79.70} = £106,650$$
(8)   Arrive at the residue after deducting grossed-up legacy:
$$£201,000 - £106,650 = £94,350$$
(9)   Calculate chargeable proprotion:
$$\tfrac{1}{2} \text{ of } £94,350 = £47,175$$
(10) The taxable estate is now the total of (7) and (9):
$$£94,350 + £47,175 = £153,825$$
(11) Tax on £153,825 is £29,030.
(12) The estate is distributed as follows:

	£
Legacy to son	85,000
Widow's share of residue	55,000
Tax	29,030
Net residue to daughter	31,970
Total estate	201,000

If the total chargeable specific gifts (whether subject to or free of tax) after cumulating any chargeable lifetime transfers, fall within the nil band, then the regrossing is not necessary.

Only tax free legacies require regrossing in this way. Only one legacy is shown here, but if there are several they are simply added together for regrossing up the total tax free legacies. Specific gifts given subject to tax are simply grossed up once.

CHAPTER 11

Post-death variations and disclaimers

Introduction

11.01 Under the estate duty provisions, unless there was a genuine dispute resulting in a compromise which was settled by a 'Deed of Family Arrangement', it was not possible to vary the distribution of a person's estate after death in such a way that it would be recognised for estate duty purposes as having been made by the deceased. However, a disclaimer was always possible provided the beneficiary had not received any benefit from the gift.

Review of wills made prior to 13 March 1975

11.02 With the introduction of capital transfer tax in the FA 1975, many wills drawn up before the introduction of that tax were drafted with a view to minimising estate duty. In particular, it was common practice for spouses to leave life interests to each other, rather than outright gifts, so as to attract the limited interest to spouse exemption, whereby tax was paid on the first death but not on the death of the surviving spouse. Further, the method of attributing reliefs was changed. This meant that many wills drawn up before the introduction of capital transfer tax, which were not subsequently changed, resulted in a higher overall tax liability than would have been achieved if the wills had been redrawn before the testator's death.

A will may be totally redrawn

11.03 Before the FA 1978 it was not entirely clear how far variations were possible, if there was no element of dispute, where persons other than beneficiaries or members of the family were introduced into the re-arrangement. The Inland Revenue's view was that if 'strangers' were introduced into the arrangement, there would be a transfer of value. This was resolved by the FA 1978, s 68, which has now been re-enacted in s 142. These provisions enable a will to be totally redrawn, or the distribution of an intestacy to be varied, to minimise tax liability. These new provisions do not require any dispute and provided they are effected within two years of death and the appropriate notice is given to the Board, the variations are deemed to have been made by the deceased. These new provisions apply in respect of variations made after 10 April 1978 but the Inland Revenue have announced that the introduction of a 'stranger' will not take a variation outside the scope of the earlier legislation (*Inland Revenue Press Release* (11 April 1978)).

Variations and disclaimers (s 142)

11.04 Where within the period of two years after a person's death—

(a) any of the dispositions (whether effected by will, under the law relating to intestacy, or otherwise) of the property comprised in his estate immediately before his death are varied; or

(b) the benefit conferred by any of those dispositions is disclaimed,

by an instrument in writing made by the persons or any of the persons who benefit or would benefit under the dispositions, then the variation or disclaimer shall be deemed to have been effected by the deceased and inheritance tax calculated on that basis.

11.05 Such a variation, however, shall not be deemed to have been one made by the deceased unless written notice to that effect is given to the Board within six months after the date of the instrument, or such longer time as the Board may allow, by—

(a) the person or persons making the instrument; and

(b) where the variation results in additional tax being payable, the personal representatives, who may only decline to join in the election if no or insufficient assets are held by them to discharge any additional tax that may be payable.

11.06 No election has to be made in the case of a disclaimer.

Method of election

Written notice within six months

11.07 The only requirement is that an election must be made in writing by the parties to the variation and, if it results in additional tax being paid by the estate, by the personal representatives. It must be made within six months of the variation (unless extended by concession).

The form of election

11.08 The election may be embodied in the variation itself or alternatively as a separate document. The advantage of incorporating the election in the variation itself is that it is not overlooked and a copy of the document need simply be sent to the appropriate authority by way of notice. However, an election should not be made as a matter of course. During the six months during which the notice of election may be made, circumstances may change, such as the precise tax position becoming clearer when, for example, figures are agreed with the district valuer. This gives an opportunity for the decision to elect to be reconsidered in the circumstances.

Separate elections for inheritance tax and capital gains tax

11.09 Separate elections can be made for inheritance tax and capital gains tax purposes, therefore careful consideration would have to be given to both taxes before an election is made. For example, a beneficiary of a property which has appreciated in value by £6,000 since the date of death and the date of the variation may decide not to elect for capital gains tax purposes, so that the original beneficiary may utilise his annual capital gains tax exemption and the re-directed beneficiary acquire the benefit of an uplifted base value in the asset.

11.10 Provided a variation is effected within two years of the death and notice given within six months of the variation, it does not matter whether or not the administration of the estate has been completed. A disclaimer cannot, of course, be made once an interest has been received.

11.11 In respect of inheritance tax, notice is given to the Capital Taxes Office and in respect of capital gains tax to the inspector of taxes for the district dealing with the deceased's tax affairs.

Property that may be redirected

11.12 A variation can be made of any property comprised in a person's estate for inheritance tax purposes immediately before his death. This would include the deceased's several share in a joint tenancy, which can therefore effectively be severed by agreement after death. It is expressly provided that excluded property is covered by s 142. Reversionary interests will therefore be included as would property situate outside the UK owned by a deceased who is domiciled outside the UK, which is a useful provision as this can be the base of tax planning [see para **11.40**].

Settled property excluded from variation but not disclaimer

11.13 Beneficial interests in possession in settled property are expressly excluded from these provisions and cannot be varied or disclaimed (s 142(5)). If such variations were possible, it would amount to permitting variation of trusts. However, by virtue of s 93, where a person disclaims an interest in settled property, provided the disclaimer is not made for a consideration of money or money's worth, no inheritance tax will be chargeable on the disclaimer.

Gifts with reservation are excluded

11.14 Although property subject to a reservation is treated as property to which the donor was beneficially entitled immediately before his death, it is specifically provided that the disposition of such property cannot be varied after death (FA 1986, Sch 19, para 24).

External consideration

11.15 The provisions of s 142 are not available if the variation or disclaimer is made for any consideration in money or money's worth other than consideration which consists of the making, in respect of another of the dispositions, of a variation or disclaimer to which s 142 applies. This is an anti-avoidance provision and it can best be illustrated with an example.

EXAMPLE
Under his will a husband leaves Blackacre worth £70,000 to his wife and Whiteacre worth £150,000 to his son. The mother and son then exchange properties, the mother paying the son £80,000 by way of full equality of exchange so that there is no transfer value. They then vary the will so that the son receives Blackacre and the mother Whiteacre, with a result that the son has effectively received Blackacre tax free but also received £80,000 from his mother tax free because the funds were paid by way of equality of exchange!

Minors

11.16 A variation can only be made affecting a person who is a minor provided his beneficial interest is increased. The interest cannot be decreased, even if the overall tax advantage would be to benefit the minor, such as the situation envisaged in para **11.37**. In these circumstances the only available course is an application to the court in pursuance of the Variation of Trust Act 1958. To overcome this problem, there seems to be no reason in principle why a power could not be incorporated in the will enabling guardians (or any other persons) to consent to a variation on behalf of beneficiaries who are minors.

Disclaimers

11.17 In the case of disclaimers, there is no two-year time limit during which an election has to be made, nor does any notice have to be given within six months or any other time to the Inland Revenue of the disclaimer. However, in practice, a disclaimer may have to be made fairly soon as, once a person has received any enjoyment or benefit from the gift, it is no longer possible to disclaim it.

11.18 Once an effective election of variation has been made, or once there has been a disclaimer, then for inheritance tax purposes variations in the estate are deemed to have been made by the deceased and are therefore retrospective to the date of death.

Income tax implications

Variation not retrospective

11.19 While a variation is retrospective to the date of death for inheritance tax purposes, this does not apply to income tax, and any income which has fallen due between the date of death and variation is deemed to be the income of the original beneficiary before the variation is made. This problem does not arise in the case of a disclaimer as a disclaimer cannot be made once any benefit from the disclaimed gift arises.

Person making the variation may be a settlor

11.20 By virtue of the TA 1970, s 454(3), a settlement includes any disposition, trust, covenant, agreement or arrangement, and the settlor is defined as any person by whom the settlement was made. By entering into a variation a settlement may therefore be created, the effect of which is that the person making the variation will be the settlor. The important implication of this is that if the variation is in favour of the settlor's child who is still a minor, any income arising from the assets varied in favour of the child will, during his minority, be taxed as the income of the parent under Taxes Act 1970, ss 437 and 438. The same problem does not seem to apply in the case of a disclaimer.

Capital gains tax implications

11.21   The provisions concerning capital gains tax are somewhat similar to those applying to inheritance tax and are contained in ss 49(6) and (7) of the Capital Gains Tax Act 1979. These provisions provide that where within two years of a person's death any of the dispositions in his estate of property of which he was competent to dispose are varied, or benefit disclaimed, by an instrument in writing made by the persons who benefit under the dispositions, the variation or disclaimer shall not constitute a disposal for capital gains tax purposes and the variations take effect as if they had been made by the deceased or, in the case of a disclaimer, had never been conferred.

Notice of election

11.22   The same provisions apply with regard to the requirement of notice in the case of a variation to inheritance tax. Again no notice is necessary in the case of a disclaimer.

Variation v Disclaimer

11.23   A beneficiary of an estate may sometimes be in a position where he can make a choice as to whether he makes a variation or disclaimer of his interest in the estate. This could arise, for example, where a beneficiary is a specific legatee and wishes his interest under the will to pass to those entitled to the residue of the estate. In this situation he can either enter into a deed of variation or simply disclaim his interest. Where this choice is available, consideration will have to be given as to which is the better alternative.

11.24   A disclaimer can only be made before the person disclaiming has taken any beneficial enjoyment from the property. Also, a disclaimer cannot re-direct the property. Further, there can only be a disclaimer of the whole of the gift if there is only one asset or if it is intended to operate as one gift.

11.25   A disclaimer does not have to be in writing, although for the purpose of treating it as a disposition having been made by the deceased under s 142, it must be made in writing within two years of the death.

Advantages of a disclaimer

11.26   The advantages of a disclaimer may be listed as follows:

(i)   a disclaimer is possible of a settled interest where no variation is possible;

(ii)   a person disclaiming an interest is not a settlor if, as a result of disclaiming his interest, it passes to his children who are minors;

(iii) a person disclaiming is not treated as having received the income between date of death and the disclaimer, although if income has been received, it is in any event too late to make a disclaimer.

A deed advisable

11.27   The variation or disclaimer must be in writing although no form is prescribed. It could be made in letter form or by any other written document. There is no requirement that it should be by deed, although if there is no consideration given by the person benefitting from the variation, any such variation could not be enforced. In this situation a deed would be advisable. In view of the fact that stamp duty on a deed of variation is now only the fixed duty of 50p, it is generally advisable to make such variations by deed.

Insertion of powers

11.28   Where the deceased has died intestate or made a home-made will, or otherwise inserted insufficient powers into the will, it may be useful to insert the usual extended powers into the variation, particularly where life interests are involved.

11.29   If all beneficiaries likely to be affected by the amended powers are of full age and capacity, these additional powers can be inserted; but if they are unable to consent, for example if they are minors, it is not possible to insert extended binding powers unless these can only be exercised exclusively for the benefit of the beneficiaries who cannot give consent.

Statement of variation in the body of the deed

11.30   It was reported in *The Law Society Gazette* (7 November 1984) that the Capital Taxes Office were adopting the view that unless a deed of variation stated in the deed itself (and not merely in a recital) that it was varying the dispositions of the deceased's property comprised in his estate immediately prior to his death or was operating as a disclaimer of the benefit of the dispositions, it would not attract the relief under s 142. This attitude caused particular problems as a precedent based on a former Form 4 in the service volume of Forms & Precedents failed to comply with this requirement.

The Inland Revenue's requirements

11.31 It is generally considered that this view was incorrect, as this requirement could not be interpreted from s 142 provided the notice of election was to that effect. As a result of the controversy which ensued, the Inland Revenue have now partially modified their stance, and their requirements will be satisfied provided:

(i) the instrument in writing is made by the persons or any of the persons who benefit or would benefit under the disposition of the property comprised in the deceased's estate immediately before his death;

(ii) the instrument is made within two years after the date of death;

(iii) the instrument clearly indicates the dispositions that are the subject of it and varies their destinations as laid down by the deceased's will, or under the law of intestacy or otherwise;

(iv) a notice of election is given within six months of the date of the instrument, unless the Board see fit to accept a late election; and

(v) the notice of election refers to the appropriate statutory provisions.

Form of election in the deed

11.32 Subject to the comments in para **11.08** as to the advisability of a separate election, the simplest way of avoiding any problems is to incorporate an election in the body of the deed itself and an accepted form is:

'By their execution of this deed the parties hereto give notice to the Board of Inland Revenue of an election that the provisions of section 142 of the Inheritance Tax Act 1984 [and of section 49(6) of the Capital Gains Tax Act 1979] shall apply to this deed so that the variation of the disposition of the estate of the deceased effected by this deed shall be deemed to be a variation effected by the deceased'.

Multiple variations

11.33 It is possible to make a series of variations relating to the same estate provided they are completed within two years of death and notice of election is given within six months. However, following the report in *The Law Society Gazette* referred to in para **11.30** above, there is now some doubt how far subsequent variations, certainly of the same property, can be made. The attitude now taken by the Capital Taxes Office is as follows:

(i) an election which is validly made is irrevocable;

(ii) a variation will not fall within s 142 if it *further* redirects any item or part of an item that has *already* been redirected under an earlier instrument; and

(iii) to avoid any uncertainty, variations covering a number of items should, ideally, be made in one instrument.

Subsequent variation of the same property now doubtful

11.34 It would therefore seem that it is no longer certain that two variations can be made in respect of the same property. It is considered that this view (ie that subsequent variations cannot be made) is wrong, as s 142(1)(A) refers to the possibility of varying any dispositions (whether effected by will, under the law relating to intestacy or *otherwise*) of the property comprised in the deceased's estate immediately before his death. This would appear to cover the subsequent variation of an earlier variation. This point can be of particular importance as, if an estate is not chargeable, for example where it has been left to an exempt transferee, the Capital Taxes Office will not agree the valuation of a property until such time as tax becomes chargeable or potentially chargeable. It has therefore been a practice to enter into a deed of variation to make the estate chargeable and hence force an agreement of value with the district valuer of, for example, a farm property and when the value has been agreed, subsequently, to vary the estate in such a way as to maximise the tax advantage. This would no longer appear to be possible unless the gift was effected by stages, for instance by giving a smaller share in the property than it is anticipated would be the final distribution, so as to compel the Inland Revenue to agree a value on the asset.

IRC v Ramsey and Furniss v Dawson

11.35 The scope of the doctrine enunciated in *IRC v Ramsey* and developed in *Furniss v Dawson* is still not entirely clear, nor, indeed, is it certain whether the principle applies to inheritance tax. Indications are that the doctrine now applies to all taxes.

The principle

11.36 To fall within the *Ramsey* principle there must be a pre-planned transaction or transactions or tax saving scheme which has no commercial purpose other than avoiding, deferring, or saving tax or obtaining a tax advantage. As most deeds of variation are entered into to minimise inheritance tax, often by way of equalising estates, it would seem in principle that they would be covered by the rule in *Furniss v Dawson*. However, if this attitude were taken, the whole purpose of the availability of deeds of variation would be defeated.

Variation solely for tax advantage

11.37 It seems, therefore, that to avoid the possibility of the rule being applied, some variation must be made which is other than for a pure tax advantage. An illustration of the variation effected purely to achieve a tax advantage is where, for example, a husband died leaving his entire estate to his wife outright or for life, and the wife subsequently dies within two years of her husband's death, leaving her entire estate to her children. Clearly this is a situation where the estates should be equalised. In such circumstances it has been normal practice for a deed of variation to be effected of the husband's estate whereby the widow's executors, with the concurrence of the children who are the beneficiaries under the widow's will, vary the husband's will to provide that half or some other part of his estate does not pass into the widow's estate but direct to the children, thereby utilising the nil or lower rate band of the husband's estate.

11.38 The ultimate destination of the assets is identical, namely the children, whether or not the deed of variation is effected. The Inland Revenue's argument is that the deed of variation serves no purpose whatsoever other than to achieve a tax saving.

Introduction of another purpose

11.39 In such circumstances it would seem advisable that the re-directed assets in the husband's estate should be to persons other than those entitled to the widow's estate or else into a form of discretionary settlement. Directing specific assets in the husband's estate to the children, or possibly varying their shares, would achieve the same purpose, particularly if there is not exact equality in the distribution.

Variation of estates of persons domiciled outside the UK

11.40 If a deceased is domiciled outside the UK at the date of his death, no inheritance tax is paid on assets unless they are situate in the UK. If such an estate is subsequently varied by means of creating a settlement within two years, such settlement will be regarded as having been made by a non-domiciled deceased. If the trustees then invest in assets outside the UK, they will be exempt from inheritance tax during the subsistence of the trust and on the death of the beneficiary, even if resident or domiciled in the UK, no inheritance tax will arise in respect of such assets. No such capital gains tax advantage arises but in any event such tax will be postponed to such time as capital is actually paid to the UK resident.

Precatory trusts (s 143)

11.41 Where a testator expresses a wish that property bequeathed by his will should be transferred by the legatee to other persons, and the legatee transfers any of the property in accordance with that wish within the period of two years after the date of death, that distribution shall take effect as if the property transferred had been bequeathed by the will to the transferee. This section therefore covers the precatory trusts often used in the case of personal chattels to overcome the problems of incorporation of documents in a will. It seems that the wishes of the testator need not even be formal or in writing (*CTT News* (July 1982)).

Discretionary wills (s 114)

11.42 By virtue of these provisions it is possible to create a discretionary trust of some or all the assets comprised in the estate. When the appointment was made or the property otherwise distributed this would normally give rise to a charge to tax. Provided, however, the appointment or distribution is made within two years of the testator's death, s 144 provides that the ultimate distribution is deemed to have been effected by the testator's will. Discretionary wills are outside the scope of this book but reference can be made to Ray *Practical Inheritance Tax Planning* (to be published by Butterworths in 1987) and Courtney *Trust Taxation Manual.*

Surviving spouse redemption of life interest (s 145)

11.43 Where on an intestacy the surviving spouse elects to commute her life interest into a capital sum, this is not treated as a transfer of value. She is treated as if, instead of being entitled to a life interest, she had been entitled to the capital sum.

Inheritance (Provision for Family and Dependants) Act 1975 (s 146)

11.44 Where an order is made under this Act, the estate is treated as if, on the deceased's death, his property devolved subject to the provisions in the order and any inheritance tax is calculated, or repaid, on that basis.

11.45 There is no time limit or notice required in such a case provided there is an order of the court. This means that if the action is settled, this can be effected by a deed of variation, but in that case notice must be given within the two-year period and an election made within six months. If more than two years have elapsed it will be necessary to obtain a consent order to bring it within the provisions of s 146.

Appendix A

Principal changes effected by the FA 1986

This appendix is intended to assist the reader in assimilating the changes effected by the FA 1986. Although for convenience the main paragraphs are summarised under each head, it is suggested that the paragraphs in the column 'Primary reading' should be read in the order shown to appraise the changes. Where appropriate, cross-references to related matters appear in the main text of the Guide.

Appendix B

INHERITANCE TAX TABLES

Commencing on 18 March 1986

Death rates

Cumulative chargeable transfers (gross) £	Rate on gross %	Tax on band £	Cumulative tax £	Cumulative chargeable transfers (net) £	Rate on net fraction
0— 71,000	0	0	0	0— 71,000	nil
71,000— 95,000	30	7,200	7,200	71,000— 87,800	3/7
95,000—129,000	35	11,900	19,100	87,800—109,900	7/13
129,000—164,000	40	14,000	33,100	109,900—130,000	2/3
164,000—206,000	45	18,900	52,000	130,900—154,000	9/11
206,000—257,000	50	25,500	77,500	154,000—179,500	1
257,000—317,000	55	33,000	110,500	179,500—206,500	1 2/9
Over 317,000	60	—	—	Over 206,500	1 1/2

Half Rates

Cumulative chargeable transfers (gross) £	Rate on gross %	Tax on band £	Cumulative tax £	Cumulative chargeable transfers (net) £	Rate on net fraction
0— 71,000	0	0	0	0— 71,000	nil
71,000— 95,000	15	3,600	3,600	71,000— 91,400	3/17
95,000—129,000	17½	5,950	9,550	91,400—119,450	7/33
129,000—164,000	20	7,000	16,550	119,450—147,450	1/4
164,000—206,000	22½	9,450	26,000	147,450—180,000	9/31
206,000—257,000	25	12,750	38,750	180,000—218,250	1/3
257,000—317,000	27½	16,500	55,250	218,250—261,750	11/29
Over 317,000	30	—	—	Over 261,750	3/7

Appendix C

CAPITAL TRANSFER TAX TABLES

6 April 1985—17 March 1986

Death rates

Cumulative chargeable transfers (gross) £	Rate on gross %	Tax on band £	Cumulative tax £	Cumulative chargeable transfers (net) £	Rate on net fraction
0— 67,000	0	nil	nil	0— 67,000	nil
67,000— 89,000	30	6,600	6,600	67,000— 82,400	$3/7$
89,000—122,000	35	11,550	18,150	82,400—103,850	$7/13$
122,000—155,000	40	13,200	31,350	103,850—123,650	$2/3$
155,000—194,000	45	17,550	48,900	123,650—145,100	$9/11$
194,000—243,000	50	24,500	73,400	145,100—169,600	1
243,000—299,000	55	30,800	104,200	169,600—194,800	$1\,2/9$
299,000 +	60	—	—	194,800 +	$1\,1/2$

Lifetime rates

Cumulative chargeable transfers (gross) £	Rate on gross %	Tax on band £	Cumulative tax £	Cumulative chargeable transfers (net) £	Rate on net fraction
0— 67,000	0	nil	nil	0— 67,000	nil
67,000— 89,000	15	3,300	3,300	67,000— 85,700	$3/17$
89,000—122,000	17½	5,775	9,075	85,700—112,925	$7/33$
122,000—155,000	20	6,600	15,675	112,925—139,325	$1/4$
155,000—194,000	22½	8,775	24,450	139,325—169,550	$9/31$
194,000—243,000	25	12,250	36,700	169,550—206,300	$1/3$
243,000—299,000	27½	15,400	52,100	206,300—246,900	$11/29$
299,000 +	30	—	—	246,900 +	$3/7$

CAPITAL TRANSFER TAX TABLES

13 March 1984—5 April 1985

Death rates

Cumulative chargeable transfers (gross)	Rate on gross	Tax on band	Cumulative tax	Cumulative chargeable transfers (net)	Rate on net fraction
£	%	£	£	£	
0— 64,000	0	nil	nil	0— 64,000	nil
64,000— 85,000	30	6,300	6,300	64,000— 78,700	$3/7$
85,000—116,000	35	10,850	17,150	78,700— 98,850	$7/13$
116,000—148,000	40	12,800	29,950	98,850—118,050	$2/3$
148,000—185,000	45	16,650	46,600	118,050—138,400	$9/11$
185,000—232,000	50	23,500	70,100	138,400—161,900	1
232,000—285,000	55	29,150	99,250	161,900—185,750	$1\frac{2}{9}$
285,000 +	60	—	—	185,750 +	$1\frac{1}{2}$

Lifetime rates

Cumulative chargeable transfers (gross)	Rate on gross	Tax on band	Cumulative tax	Cumulative chargeable transfers (net)	Rate on net fraction
£	%	£	£	£	
0— 64,000	0	nil	nil	0— 64,000	nil
64,000— 85,000	15	3,150	3,150	64,000— 81,850	$3/17$
85,000—116,000	17½	5,425	8,575	81,850—107,425	$7/33$
116,000—148,000	20	6,400	14,975	107,425—133,025	$1/4$
148,000—185,000	22½	8,325	23,300	133,025—161,700	$9/31$
185,000—232,000	25	11,750	35,050	161,700—196,950	$1/3$
232,000—285,000	27½	14,575	49,625	196,950—235,375	$11/29$
285,000 +	30	—	—	235,375 +	$3/7$

CAPITAL TRANSFER TAX TABLES

15 March 1983—23 March 1984

Death rates

Cumulative chargeable transfers (gross)	Rate on gross	Tax on band	Cumulative tax	Cumulative chargeable transfers (net)	Rate on net fraction
£	%	£	£	£	
0— 60,000	0	nil	nil	0— 60,000	nil
60,000— 80,000	30	6,000	6,000	60,000— 74,000	3/7
80,000— 110,000	35	10,500	16,500	74,000— 93,500	7/13
110,000— 140,000	40	12,000	28,500	93,500—111,500	2/3
140,000— 175,000	45	15,750	44,250	111,500—130,750	9/11
175,000— 220,000	50	22,500	66,750	130,750—153,250	1
220,000— 270,000	55	27,500	94,250	153,250—175,750	1 2/9
270,000— 700,000	60	258,000	352,250	175,750—347,750	1 1/2
700,000—1,325,000	65	406,250	758,500	347,750—566,500	1 6/7
1,325,000—2,650,000	70	927,500	1,686,000	566,500—964,000	2 1/3
2,650,000 +	75	—	—	964,000 +	3

Lifetime rates

Cumulative chargeable transfers (gross)	Rate on gross	Tax on band	Cumulative tax	Cumulative chargeable transfers (net)	Rate on net fraction
£	%	£	£	£	
0— 60,000	0	nil	nil	0— 60,000	nil
60,000— 80,000	15	3,000	3,000	60,000— 77,000	3/17
80,000— 110,000	17½	5,250	8,250	77,000— 101,750	7/33
110,000— 140,000	20	6,000	14,250	101,750— 125,750	1/4
140,000— 175,000	22½	7,875	22,125	125,750— 152,875	9/31
175,000— 220,000	25	11,250	33,375	152,875— 186,625	1/3
220,000— 270,000	30	15,000	48,375	186,625— 221,625	3/7
270,000— 700,000	35	150,500	198,875	221,625— 501,125	7/13
700,000—1,325,000	40	250,000	448,875	501,125— 876,125	2/3
1,325,000—2,650,000	45	596,250	1,045,125	876,125—1,604,875	9/11
2,650,000 +	50	—	—	1,604,875 +	1

Index